WHAT PEOPLE ARE SAYING ABOUT
JOYFULLY AGING: A CHRISTIAN'S GUIDE

Aging! It's something we all do effortlessly and without exception. Some do it gracefully, even elegantly, others by whimpering and wailing in protest. You know the sorts who actually answer the question "How are you?" by giving an organ recital—the anatomical, not musical version—when the only polite answer to that query is "Fine," however great the fib. For all who have a hard time dealing with years that should truly be golden in the best sense, Rich Bimler comes to the rescue in these pages with his trademark blend of wit, wisdom, and worship. A gifted Christian humorist and wordsmith, Bimler examines aging now that he is also a happy victim of the phenomenon, and he delivers delightful therapy for all who try to resist. Read these pages and—improbable to imagine!—you may even enjoy the aging process.

Paul L. Maier, author, educator, LCMS vice-president

Joyfully Aging is not only the title of Richard Bimler's latest book but is a synopsis of its content as well—plus a delightful description of the author's own life moment. In forty-six crisply written chapters Richard let's us in on the joy he has found throughout the aging process and shines his unique light of humorous insight onto a period of life so misunderstood by many. Richard shows us how God means aging to be a joyful, life long process. One way God does this is by reserving the gift of grandchildren until we are old enough to appreciate and enjoy the blessings of youth. Richard helps us get into that frame of mind.

Charles S. Mueller, Sr., pastor emeritus of Trinity Lutheran
Church, Roselle, Illinois

Sometimes incisive, sometimes insightful, frequently humorous, but always Gospel centered. Each chapter lets the reader hear the confession of an aging pilgrim who shares his thoughts and reflections about aging gracefully, graciously and gratefully. Here you have a Christian guide for celebrating God's gift of aging . . . a resource book for personal edification, for discussion groups, for suggestions in mentoring the next generation.

Rev. Walter M. Schoedel, Director of Church Relations for
Lutheran Senior Services of Missouri and Illinois and pastor emeritus of
Concordia Lutheran Church, Kirkwood, Missouri

We have no choice in growing old, but we can choose how we live our later years. Rich Bimler invites us to experience growing older as a spiritual passage. He engages the reader with spiritual insights and a positive, hopeful attitude. He is a master storyteller, showing us how to make sense of the aging experience and how to live with courage and meaning. This gem of a book will delight, encourage, and inspire all readers.

Joyfully Aging is another example of Rich Bimler's wonderful ability to encourage people of all ages to live in the joy of the Resurrection. Joyfully Aging is a celebration of the gifts of aging and of the importance of the Christian family, delivered with the stories and unique humor for which Rich is known and loved. Readers will come away reminded of who they are, whose they are, and the endless possibilities for lives of service and relevance made possible by God's grace. Thanks, Rich!

In *Joyfully Aging,* Rich urges us to get rid of gloomy despair and re-focus on the reality of the risen Lord and our resurrection life, the true source of joy!

A profound biblical truth underlies *Joyfully Aging:* while the devil and his minions would wipe the smile from our faces, the world can laugh again, for despair is replaced by the joy of salvation in Jesus, the risen One! Pointing us to that reality, Rich encourages people of all ages to share the Good News that alone can lift hearts and spirits!

Thanks, Rich! Good theology! Good humor!

Rev. Dr. Thomas R. Zehnder, pastor, president emeritus, Florida-Georgia District, LCMS, executive director, LCMS World Mission (retired)

Dr. Rich Bimler's wit, wisdom, and inspiration shine through on every page of *Joyfully Aging.* Using Scripture as constant touchstone, Dr. Bimler (or "Rich," as people all over the world know him) provides an antidote to our youth obsessed culture with a perspective on aging as a time to reflect, mentor, laugh, connect, and pray. What a treasure for old and young alike."

David Walsh, Ph.D., psychologist, author, and speaker

JOYFULLY AGING
A CHRISTIAN'S GUIDE

JOYFULLY AGING

A CHRISTIAN'S GUIDE

RICHARD BIMLER

AMBASSADOR OF HEALTH, HOPE AND AGING

CONCORDIA PUBLISHING HOUSE · SAINT LOUIS

Published by Concordia Publishing House
3558 S. Jefferson Avenue, St. Louis, MO 63118-3968
1-800-325-3040 · www.cph.org

Manufactured in the United States of America

Library of Congress Cataloging-in-Publication Data

Bimler, Richard.

 Joyful aging : a Christian's guide / Richard Bimler.

   p. cm.

 Includes bibliographical references and index.

 ISBN 978-0-7586-3772-7 (alk. paper)

 1. Older Christians--Religious life. 2. Aging--Religious aspects--Christianity. I. Title.

 BV4580.B53 2012

 248.8'5--dc23   2012015297

3 4 5 6 7 8 9 10   21 20 19 18 17 16 15 14 13

DEDICATION:

This book on celebrating the gift of aging is dedicated
  ❈ to my grandparents, who always seemed old to me;
  ❈ to my parents, who never seemed old to me; and
  ❈ to my grandchildren—Matt, Rachel, Hannah,
    Sarah, Aaron, Emma, and Abbey—who continue
    to bless Hazel and me with celebrating God's gift
    of aging from generation to generation!

TABLE OF CONTENTS

Introduction		12
Chapter 1:	Reflections for Older Adults	15
Chapter 2:	The Attitude of Aging	17
Chapter 3:	We Are "Aha" People in the Lord!	21
Chapter 4:	So What Term Do We Use to Describe "Aging People"?	25
Chapter 5:	Telling His Story While Telling Our Story	29
Chapter 6:	Aging: It's All about the Alpha and Omega	33
Chapter 7:	Laughter and Aging Go Together like a Horse and Carriage	37
Chapter 8:	Laughter: A Gift for All Ages, Especially the Old	40
Chapter 9:	Wit, Wisdom, Wrinkles, and Wows	44
Chapter 10:	Aging Gracefully: Hope or Hype?	48
Chapter 11:	Thank God I'm Old!	53
Chapter 12:	The Three Rs of Aging	56
Chapter 13:	Amazing Grays	62
Chapter 14:	"Aha" Moments	66
Chapter 15:	The D and A of Aging	71
Chapter 16:	Preparing for Aging	76
Chapter 17:	Put Your Blinkers On	83
Chapter 18:	Keeping Our Aging Bodies Well	87
Chapter 19:	Looking for Hope in All the Right Places	91
Chapter 20:	The Real World Health Organization	96
Chapter 21:	The Aging-Friendly Church	100
Chapter 22:	Mattering and Mentoring	108

Chapter 23: Our Changing Role as We Grow Older   112

Chapter 24: EncourAGE, EncourAGE, EncourAGE!   119

Chapter 25: Down with Groan-Ups!   126

Chapter 26: Okay, What Is So Good about Aging?   131

Chapter 27: Leaving a Legacy: For Others or in Others?   138

Chapter 28: Grandparenting Is Grand   142

Chapter 29: Living in a Different County Together and Speaking a Different Language   150

Chapter 30: The Generation Gap Revisited   157

Chapter 31: Who Says Older Adults Are Technologically Challenged?   162

Chapter 32: That's What Friends Are For   168

Chapter 33: Older Adults: The Ministering Ones   173

Chapter 34: Go Ye Forth . . . and Connect!   180

Chapter 35: Taking the Risk   185

Chapter 36: Look at All the Famous Older People!   189

Chapter 37: Paraprosdokians and Aging   195

Chapter 38: Downsizing? No, Upsizing!   200

Chapter 39: Wee, We, Whee—All the Way Home!   204

Chapter 40: Once More with Attitude   208

Chapter 41: An Aging Litany   213

Chapter 42: Pains, Perceptions, and Promise   217

Chapter 43: Dying Well   221

Chapter 44: Got Change?   228

Chapter 45: A Call to Change the Way We Age   235

Chapter 46: A Postscript (Or, "Gee, I Wish I Had Included These Thoughts Sooner!")   244

INTRODUCTION

If there is one thing we are all doing together in this life, it's aging!

We are all aging! More of us are growing older. And more of us are growing older, longer.

So, what are you and I going to do about it?

Answering this question is what this book is all about. It is about celebrating God's gift of aging instead of moaning and complaining about old age. It is about seeing aging as a blessing instead of a burden. It is about affirming life as a gift from God, despite all of our worries and woes and wrinkles and whining. It is about living an abundant life in the Lord here as we anticipate the eternal life that Christ proclaims to us as the reason for His coming.

This book is not an answer book. It will not tell you what to do to make the rest of your years fine and dandy. It will not rid you of your problems, pains, and pouting. It will not tell you that things are going to get better in your life if you only shape up and live right.

But it will promise that you and I will live "happily ever after" because of the promise we have in Jesus Christ! Through our Baptism, God in Christ has marked us with water and the sign of the cross. By faith, we are His people forever, whether we are fifteen, fifty-five, seventy-five, or beyond. Mark 16:16 assures us that "whoever believes and is baptized will be saved." God promises believers that He will never leave us, therefore, we can affirm that we will live "happily ever after" in Him, in heaven, forever!

I have been preparing to write this book all seventy-two years of my life. However, I could not have written it any sooner because I did not have the experiences and relationships that I have now. These experiences and relationships have helped me make better sense of the aging process. For me, as it has no doubt been for you, life has been a roller coaster ride of Good Fridays and Easters, all mixed together. Just like you, I have experienced many low and dark times throughout my years as well as many high and lighthearted times. I have been frustrated as I struggled with fears and failures and foibles, and I have celebrated life through affirming people around me and the love and forgiveness of people whom God placed very strategically in my life.

Although I have been planning to write this book all these years, I was not ready to articulate my journey until now. I am slowly learning to better understand my earlier years through these later years as I reflect, discern, and mentor others in the process. And I hope that through these pages, I can communicate my perspective to you—

that a truly satisfying life story is possible only when we learn from life's experiences, all of its "uh-ohs" and its "aha's," when we keep Christ at the center.

So enjoy the journey of aging well each day in the Lord. As Romans 14:8 reminds us, "If we live, we live to the Lord, and if we die, we die to the Lord. So then, whether we live or whether we die, we are the Lord's."

Thank You, Lord, for allowing us to live another day in You! Yes, indeed, aging is the only way to live!

CHAPTER ONE

REFLECTIONS FOR OLDER ADULTS

As you move through these pages, feel free to make notes, skip chapters, and bounce around in order to have fun reading this resource. Here is one way to get you started as you think about aging.

Fill in the blanks and discuss the following thoughts:

1. One thing I like about being old is _____
_____.

2. Just because I'm over sixty doesn't mean I can't
_____.

3. When I was young, one person who supported and encouraged me was _____
by doing_____.

4. The best thing I can do for someone younger than me is to _____.

5. One thing I still want to do in life is _____
_____.

6. Being old is a _____
experience.

7. What I like about myself right now is _____

_____

_____

8. One gift that I can give to someone younger than me
   is _____

_____

9. Something I did in my childhood that I am glad I
   did was _____

_____

10. Today, I thank God for my life because _____

_____

_____

Share your thoughts and reflections with someone else. Sit and talk with a youngster about your outlook and perspective on life, using these sentences as a starting point. Enjoy the discussion!

CHAPTER TWO

THE ATTITUDE OF AGING

Aging is a gift and a blessing. To accept each day as a gift from the Lord is to celebrate Christ's presence within us. In contrast, to see aging as a burden, a problem, or a chore is to deny what the Lord gives to us each day: a new life in Him!

I have a friend (at least two of them!) who likes to say, "My goal in life is to live forever! And so far, so good!" Well, bless him for his positive attitude, but some day . . . !

I shared many experiences of life with another friend, the sainted Herb Brokering. There were times during our trips to other countries when we were not sure if we would survive the situations in which we found ourselves. On one especially dreary evening, we talked about life and we talked about death. That day, we made a promise to each other that both of us would speak at the other's funeral service! Well, in November 2009, I kept my promise and shared parts of Herb's life at his funeral. We'll just have to wait to see if Herb shows up at my funeral!

The point of these stories is that our attitude toward life is a key ingredient to the aging process. Seeing life as something to control, to get by with, or to last forever is quite foolish, obviously. Seeing life as something to endure, to make the most of, or to live with all the gusto you can is not at all centering on why the Lord gave us life in the first place.

I remember my days as a youngster—I was nine or ten at the time—when my mom said something like this to me: "Richie, this is the best time of your life. It doesn't get any better!" I remember looking at her and thinking, "Yikes; if this is the best time of my life, I am in trouble!"

We live in a culture that still honors and worships youth. People still want to look youthful, smell youthful, and talk youthful. Those things aren't bad if you are a teenager! But why sweat the wrinkles? Why worry about not being able to play three-on-three basketball or to run ten miles a day? Instead, why not work at being the most joy-filled person in the world, or at least in your neighborhood, as a _____-year-old (you fill in your age)?

I love the Japanese inscription on the wall of the hospice center at the Lutheran Medical Center in Wheat Ridge, Colorado. It states, "The setting sun is no less beautiful than the rising sun." How true, how true!

To celebrate aging in no way denies the joys and opportunities of being young. Developing an aging attitude toward life actually affirms life at every age! And that's just the point. Throughout Scripture, we do not hear much about people of different ages sitting or standing around and talking about aging, do we? Instead, we read about young people (such as Mary, the mother of Jesus, for example) and older folks such as Abraham, Anna, and Noah, and on and on, who went about serving the Lord, listening to the Lord, and celebrating the Lord's presence in their lives. Now that is what I call an attitude of aging!

Still another challenge we have as we age is the notion that we have now earned our chance to retire. We've been there, done that. We can now, finally, take it easy, go fishing and golfing when we want to, and relax, because we've paid the price. Remember the comic strip that has Grandma asking Grandpa, "What are you going to do today?" Grandpa says, "Nothing." "I thought you did that yesterday," responds Grandma. "That's right," he says, "but I didn't finish!"

There is no such thing as retiring on this side of heaven. We leave jobs, we reposition from one area of focus to another, and we transition between places and people, but we never retire. It is not a concept shared in the Scriptures. Numbers 8:25 does say, "From the age of fifty years they shall withdraw from the duty of the service and serve no more." In context, this verse talks more about the role of the person transitioning from one role to another of serving as a mentor or coach to younger people. The writer continues by encouraging these older people to assist the young people in the tasks at hand.

Unfortunately, our society has convinced people that after a certain age, be it fifty or sixty-five or even later, people lose their significance and purpose in life because of their age. The Church, however, is the one place where people of all ages come together around Word and Sacrament to proclaim to one another that Jesus Christ is Lord of all—and that includes all ages!

I'd say we have our work cut out for us. I hope you agree.

CHAPTER THREE

WE ARE "AHA" PEOPLE IN THE LORD!

I love my title as the *A*mbassador of *H*ealth, *H*ope, and *A*ging (or "AH-HA"!) with Lutheran Life Communities in Arlington Heights, Illinois. My role is to speak on behalf of older adults and encourage and affirm older adult ministries in congregations.

The really good news about this is that I am not the only "aha" person around; we all are "aha" people because of Christ's death and resurrection for us. The resurrection is the biggest "aha" of all! Because of this fact, you and I are empowered to be "aha" people to ourselves and to those around us.

Notice the affirming words from the apostle John in 1 John 3:1: "See what kind of love the Father has given to us, that we should be called children of God; and so we are." John means exactly what he says: God in Christ loves us all, right now, today, tomorrow, and forever. He loves us even when we do not look like it or act like it or even feel like it. Our faith does not depend on how we act, look, or feel. It all depends on the fact that Christ Jesus died and rose again for you and for me!

We can think about this truth another way by remembering that we are *nouns* before we are *verbs*. I often get this mixed up. Too often, I try to do something for someone to prove my worthiness, rather than getting it in my head that first I am someone in Christ, and because I am His, I am then able to do things for myself and others.

We are "be do, be do" people of God: Because He first loved us human *be*ings, by His love and grace, we are now empowered to *do* His work in service and care for others. Colossians 3 affirms us as "aha" people of God by revealing that through faith in Christ Jesus, we are God's people and are therefore enabled by the Spirit to embrace all of the wonderful qualities that the Spirit bestows on us: compassion, kindness, humility, forgiveness, gentleness, and patience—and many more!

"Aha" people come in all shapes, sizes, and ages too. Older adults share their "aha" experiences with young children. Little children become "aha" people to us seventy-year-olds through their joy and laughter. Watch for a chance to become an "aha" person to a teenager through a word of encouragement or just a wink. Remember to watch for times when teenagers (yes, even teenagers!) bring a smile to your face and a "well done" to your lips for something they say or do.

What the world needs now is not a lot of "no" and "wait" and "don't" and "watch it." What the world needs now is a lot of "aha" and "yes" and "hooray" and "way to go" from older "aha" people to younger "aha" people.

However, this also has to be said: If you are like me, and I'm guessing you are, then you and I do get caught in our "uh-oh" days. These are the days when things do not go well, when people get angry at us, and when we're not easy to live with either. There are days when you and I are not all that affirming or helpful or caring toward others around us. There are days when we feel like saying, "In case of an accident, I'm not surprised." There are days when I throw a pity party for myself, and I assume that no one will show up except me.

I call these "uh-oh" days my "Good Friday" days. These are days when I really do not feel very good about myself, not to mention my disdain and disappointment of others. On these days, what I need are "aha" people, resurrection resources, to be with me and to point me from the Good Friday of the cross to the empty tomb of Easter.

Moreover, on days when I am feeling and living like an "aha" person, full of joy and energy for the Lord, myself, and others, I am happy to share my faith in the Lord with people around me who are stuck in their "uh-oh" Good Fridays. The Lord has put all of us in ministry range of one another so we might build each other up as the Body of Christ. This truth becomes even more meaningful when we realize that God puts each of us in families and con-gregations and communities where there are people of all ages. We were not meant to hang around only with our own peer group! You and I need to rub ministry shoulders with six-year-olds and sixteen-year-olds. Believe it or not, six- and sixteen-year-olds need us sixty-six-and-older people to talk with as well.

When was the last time you actually had a conversation with someone forty years younger or older than you? Perhaps today is the day!

Go for it, you "aha" person of God!

CHAPTER FOUR

SO WHAT TERM DO WE USE TO DESCRIBE "AGING PEOPLE"?

All people are aging people. To live is to age. However, after these two agreed-upon statements, the discussion gets far more heated!

I am amazed, at least sometimes, at how uncomfortable are some people over fifty at using the term *old* to describe their age. "No, I'm not old, I'm mature," or "Old? Not me. Sixty-five is the new forty," or, "*Old*: that sounds so . . . old!" And on and on.

This is not a new problem. As a matter of fact, the same people turning sixty-five in these years are the same people whom we couldn't figure out what to call fifty years earlier! In the early to mid sixties, discussions rolled on about whether we should call these people the youth or teenagers or kids or young people or young adults. Neither the debate nor the focus of the debate has changed, only the terms.

Through the years, we even called our friends and acquaintances different names, am I right? Did you have a nickname when you were young? I did. My nickname was Idge, but I do not want to discuss it at this point!

Even famous people may be called by a different name

as they age. Remember Billy the Kid? He is aging well and living somewhere in southwest Florida, but now his friends call him "Willie the Geezer"!

A quick survey of congregations shows that many different names are used for their older adult groups as well: S.A.G.E.S., Joy Group, Wise Ones, Senior Adult Group (or SAG), Fifty-plus, Prime Timers, OWLs (Old Walther Leaguers), Encore, Second Chance, PPPs (People of Passion and Purpose), and Senior Saints Alive.

So, how about you and your peers? Choose which category fits best for you:

☐ Seniors   ☐ Older Adults

☐ Geezers   ☐ Old Folks

☐ Retirees   ☐ Golden Agers

☐ Silver Streaks   ☐ Old Fogies

☐ None of the above

Perhaps this discussion can lead us to a few observations. First, is it really that important to name this age group? Second, according to when we were born, we are all locked in to our own definable generation, which we will never escape. Good. Live with it and in it! Enjoy the ride, regardless of your age!

It seems as though our Church, as well as our society, is once again caught in the habit of assigning everyone to a certain slot. We did this to people when they were young, and we continue to do so as they grow older. We still attempt to program people in congregations into their little slots: children here, young folks there, young married couples over there, older folks in the rockers, and so on. All along, we overlook the significance of having people of different ages together, rubbing ministry shoulders with one another.

I continue to be amazed at how the Scriptures characterize age groups. It talks about generations declaring God's Word to other generations. Joel 1:3 says we should "tell [our] children of it, and let [our] children tell their children, and their children to another generation." Psalm 100:5 sums it up so well: "For the LORD is good; His steadfast love endures forever, and His faithfulness to all generations."

So what are we saying and learning in all of this? In my opinion, go ahead and continue to minister to and with people in small groups and large groups. Go ahead and provide opportunities, big and small, for people of all ages. And as we do this, let us also be intentional about bringing people of all ages together around the Word and Sacrament, in local and international mission projects, in sharing their faith one-on-one, in visiting people in hospitals and who are homebound, and in all other ways in which the Spirit leads us.

However, in addition to all of the above, let us also

hear God's Word from Isaiah 43:1, which says, loudly and strongly, "Fear not, for I have redeemed you; I have called you by name, you are Mine."

My ninety-six-year-old friend, Adolph, had it right all along. On a recent visit, I asked him what name he preferred to be called, such as senior, older adult, or something else. He responded simply, "Just call me Adolph!"

If that's good enough for Adolph, it's good enough for me.

CHAPTER FIVE

TELLING HIS STORY WHILE TELLING OUR STORY

Consider this: Perhaps the Lord is allowing us older people to live longer on earth so we can have more opportunities to share our faith in the Lord with more people. Intriguing thought, isn't it?

Let us take it for granted that this is the Lord's plan. Let's help each other "tell the story . . . of Jesus and His love" ("I Love to Tell the Story," A. Katherine Hankey, 1866). I sure wish someone would write a hymn about it!

That was the tongue-in-cheek comment I made a few years ago at a pastors' conference in Michigan. I asked, "Why doesn't someone write a stanza for older adults about sharing our faith with others?" Here is what Pastor Tim Azzum handed to me after my presentation. (At least he used my presentation time wisely!)

> We love to tell the story
> That Jesus is the Way.
> It gives us all a reason
> To live another day.
>
> In every generation,

> Each age, its story tells
> Of how our God is faithful
> To people aging well!

What a great statement of faith for older adults! The Lord gives us added years of life so we can share and celebrate our faith in the Lord Jesus. If we are not telling the story, who is?

Dr. David Walsh of "Mind Positive Parenting" puts it this way: "Whoever tells the stories defines the culture." Ask yourself, "Who is telling the story to people young and old today, in your neighborhood and community? What is the story they are telling?" We might honestly answer by saying it is the television shows, the commercials, the songs, the movies, the front-page headlines, the political promises. It is all these and more that are telling the stories of what life is all about. Unfortunately, what their life is all about is not what a life in Jesus Christ is all about!

I am not in any way suggesting that we bad-mouth popular stars of today or throw out our flat-screen TVs or banish popular music from our homes, but I am saying that the story we have of Jesus Christ is a story of love and forgiveness and joy because Christ has come for all of us, young and old alike. He has come to us, not by saying no to us, despite our sins; rather, He has come to us saying yes because of what He has done for us in His death and resurrection. Paul says it well: "As surely as God is faithful, our word to you has not been Yes and No. For the Son of God, Jesus Christ, whom we proclaimed among you, Silvanus and Timothy and I, was not Yes and No, but in Him it is always Yes" (2 Corinthians 1:18–19).

We are yes people in the Lord! Older adults are called to be encouragers, affirmers, and cheerleaders in the Lord! True, young people need to know right from wrong; they need to see their sins and repent of them, just like adults. However, one of the many gifts older adults have as we age is the knowledge and the experience to know that we have a Lord who will never forsake us. We have a Lord who has seen us through all of our "uh-oh" days of pains and problems and pettiness. We know about this Lord who gives to all of us, young and old, His promise of life everlasting.

His story comes alive in us as we tell younger people our story of God's love and forgiveness for us. His story becomes our story as we model and talk about our memories and remembrances of God working through our sin-filled lives. We tell this story not because we have to but because we get to! That is the joy of living a life in the Lord.

Here are some questions to start us thinking more specifically about what story we want to tell and to whom we want to tell it. Add some of your own. Share these with others, especially family members and friends close to you:

    1. What is it that I want my family and friends to know about my faith, my core values, and my life's experiences?

2. For what do I wish to be remembered?

3. What blessings, stories, and traditions do I want to leave with my loved ones?

4. What can I do now to celebrate life in the Lord to enable my family to continue the celebration in their lifetime?

5. What can I do today that will help me to live out the telling of my stories to others?

Celebrate every day by telling the story of Jesus and His love in your own way. He has blessed each of us with faith in Jesus Christ. We get to share it in many ways with younger and older people around us. What a gift! What a joy to shout out and live out our faith. What a God!

Psalm 145:4 says it this way: "One generation shall commend Your works to another." That's good enough for me.

CHAPTER SIX

AGING: IT'S ALL ABOUT THE ALPHA AND OMEGA

Aging is the only way to live because growing in the Lord is the only way to live! As others have said, we live in the dash between the dates on our tombstones. Have you visited a cemetery lately? It is a good place to think about aging. Some of the saints before us lived only a few years. Others hit the one-hundred mark. Cemeteries help us to remember, rejoice, and reflect on life in the Lord.

Cemeteries can help us laugh at life as well. You, too, have seen tombstones that reflect the humor and humanity of our lives, such as the one that reads, "Here lies Herman. He was a good friend and a wonderful father, but a bad electrician." Or how about this one: "Rest in peace, Margaret. Now you are in the Lord's hands. (Lord, watch Your wallet!)" Here's one more: "Here rests George. A memory from all of your sons except Bruce, who did not pay any money!"

I saw a photo recently of a man sitting on a John Deere tractor, mowing the grass in a cemetery. It must have been during the Easter season (isn't every season the Easter season?), because he was mowing around a big sign that read,

"It is finished!" After thinking about that photo, I started chuckling about the juxtaposition of the man finishing cutting the grass and that Easter proclamation. I could just hear the caretaker, upon finishing his mowing task, shout, "Wow, I cut the grass. It is finished!"

All too often, whatever age we are, we assume that we have finished our jobs too. We did it! After twenty-five years, we got our gold watch. After thirty years of teaching, no more kids to teach. (We might even think that after just one year of teaching!) The whole point of life is to live in those dashes, the dashes between life and death, to the glory of God—because it is finished. Christ has died and risen for us! It is finished! He did it! It is not about you or about me or about us. Life is about Him: God in Jesus Christ.

That is why I like the following statement. Read it aloud to see if you can. Then think about the term, "It is finished!"

IT'S ALL AOUBT THEE
APHLA ADN OEAMGA

"Aoccdrnig to rseearch at Cmabrigde Uinervristy, it deosn't mttaer in what order the ltteers in a wrod aer; the olny iprmoatnt tihng is taht the frist and lsat ltteer be at the rghit pclae. The rset can be a tatol mses and you can slitl raed it wouthit a porbelm. This is bcuseae the huamn mnid deos not raed ervey lteter by istlef but the wrod as a wlohe."

Amzanig, huh?

This little quote points to the fact that as long as the first letter and the last letter in a word are correct, our minds can usually figure out what word it is even when the letters in between are all messed up. Now, isn't that what grace is all about? As long as we know where we have come from (our alpha) and where we are going (our omega), we understand who we are and whose we are.

Too often, we get so caught up in all those little messes we make in life, between our alpha and our omega. We worry so much about getting each letter in our lives perfect that we forget that God in Christ Jesus has already forgiven us, even when we mess things up. Perhaps even worse, we think that our faith depends on us getting all As on the spelling test of life instead of knowing, through faith, that He has already forgiven us.

Our Baptism tells us and reassures us every day that we are Christ's forgiven and redeemed people. And our Omgea, oops, Omega, affirms that we are the Lord's in death as well! Revelation 22:13 says it even better: "I am the Alpha and the Omega, the first and the last, the beginning and the end."

Enjoy this day as an alpha-and-omega day in the Lord, and forget about how well you did in spelling in school!

(Note: Can you imagine the frustration the typesetter had in printing out the quote above? My computer kept telling me, "No such word! No such word!" There must be a message there somewhere!)

CHAPTER SEVEN

LAUGHTER AND AGING GO TOGETHER LIKE A HORSE AND CARRIAGE

"Start every morning with a smile—
and get it over with!"

Now, some of you readers are already asking, "What is a horse and carriage?" If you are not sure, ask someone who is older than you for the answer.

I love to laugh. It is one of God's great gifts to all people. I sure do not agree with our friend Mr. Fields, above. Yes, it is a great thing to start each day with a smile and even a laugh, but not to "get it over with." Instead, we smile and laugh because we know how life turns out. Remember, we live on this side of the resurrection!

However, just like all gifts from God, we can misuse them just as much as we use them. Humor is misused when we laugh *at* people instead of *with* people. I take humor very seriously. It is affirming when older people laugh, especially at themselves, because it models that they are taking God very seriously while at the same time taking themselves very lightly. So, people of God, lighten up!

The phrase "Lighten up!" is not a command but rather

an affirmation from the Lord that He is in control of our lives, even when we do not think so. To "lighten up" is to remember that Jesus is the light of the world, as our smiles and grins and even guffaws shine out to others. "Lighten up" is a call to all of God's lighthearted people, reminding us that Jesus Christ has won the victory over sin and the devil.

I would like to suggest that laughter is our bold statement to the world that we are not fighting alone in our battles of sin and selfishness. We are not alone to deal with all of our problems of dysfunction and chaos around us. We have a Lord who has accepted us as we are and forgives us in all.

Perhaps people who do not laugh or smile very much not only take themselves too seriously but have also even forgotten about God. The "aha" of Easter also trumps the "uh-oh" of Good Friday.

We all remember the infamous day of 9/11. Our lives seemed to stop suddenly in their places. Our mindsets were shaken. Our hopes were drained. Everything seemed lost. A television comedian announced that all of the late-night talk shows would be cancelled indefinitely because of the 9/11 disasters. All Broadway plays were cancelled as well, because, as one commentator shared, "How could plays and shows go on, because laughter died on 9/11?"

However, as horrible as that day was, you and I need to

affirm that laughter really was not destroyed on that day. No, laughter actually died on that first Good Friday, when Christ Jesus hung on the cross for you and me. It was indeed the end of joy and hope and life itself.

But hooray and aha, our story does not end there! You and I know that laughter did not stay dead and buried. Instead, life, laughter, and celebration were resurrected in our Lord and Savior, Jesus Christ, on that first Easter morning. That is why we can sing and shout and, yes, even laugh at death. We can laugh with others because we know that we live as Easter people, and *alleluia* is our song.

Psalm 126:3 puts it so well: "The LORD has done great things for us; we are glad" This says it all. Christ has done it—He has conquered death—and our response is to be filled with joy and hope and the power of the Spirit in celebrating life in the name of the resurrected One!

And now, let's talk more about how aging and laughter go together so well, just like a horse and a carriage.

CHAPTER EIGHT

LAUGHTER: A GIFT FOR ALL AGES, ESPECIALLY THE OLD

What makes something funny? Great question!

I contend that humor is being able to see and sense the incongruities of life. We laugh because we have been there. We can identify with a story or joke or quip. The premise I would like to test in this chapter is that the older we get, the more we become aware and conscious of the incongruities of life; therefore, older people are more able to laugh and chuckle about their own weaknesses, failures, and even disappointments.

Another point about the joy of aging is that we learn to laugh at ourselves more. It becomes a daily "holy habit" for many of us. Do you ever doubt that God has a sense of humor? If you ever are having one of those days, just look in the mirror! That clears things up very quickly!

Hazel and I have been married for more than fifty years—and that is in a row. It is all by the grace of God, as we have muddled and mingled and muddied through many Good Fridays together. We are thankful that we learned early on, through wonderful mentors and forgiving friends, that one of the key ingredients to any marriage and to any relationship is the ability to laugh at ourselves and with each other. One of our favorite quips is to share that there are three major ways that the Lord has kept us together all these years:

1. We laugh a lot together;

2. We forgive a lot together; and

3. I travel a lot.

So, let's get serious about humor. I have learned—slowly, of course—that it is better for me to laugh first at myself and then at other things in life. I like to laugh at myself, because there is plenty to laugh at. Why spend time laughing at what others are doing, when individually we invent so much good material on our own?

Second, I like to laugh with older people, because I am one. Why pick on young people when we old folks do so many weird things anyway? Third, I like to laugh about Lutherans, because I am one. Sure, there are plenty of Methodists and Presbyterians around who do funny things too, but I really like to point at and pick fun at us Lutherans, especially German Lutherans (or, as the oxymoron states, us "Joy-mans").

For example, I like to tell the story about the time I approached Concordia Publishing House with a great idea for a new book. It would be all about the humor of the Lutheran Church. I even suggested the format for it. It would be printed on a 3 × 5 card, one side only. (For some reason, I never did hear again from that editor!)

Here is a top fifteen list developed by my son Bob, which is just one example of being willing and able to laugh at ourselves:

15. You wake up yelling, "Bingo"!

14. You forget where you parked your car—and you are at home.

13. You brush your teeth with Preparation H.

12. You have more hair in your ears and nose than on your head.

11. You get tired just waking up.

10. "Chewing gum" now just means that you forgot to put in your teeth.

9. If you pull your pants up any higher, you will have to keep the zipper open in order to see.

8. You sit in front of the microwave waiting for a clearer picture.

7. You believe that GPS stands for "Going Places Slowly."

6. You take more naps than your grandkids.

5. You have more spots than a leopard.

4. Your favorite drink is prune juice on the rocks.

3. You forget your children's names but can re-member when *Jeopardy!* is on television.

2. You have to store all of your medicine in a walk-in closet.

1. The first word you taught your first grandchild was "Huh?"

(Bob Bimler, Seward, Nebraska)

Yes, laughter is a gift for all ages, and especially for older adults. One of the best ways to share our faith with those younger than we are is to be able to laugh at ourselves. By doing so, we model for younger people that life is all about celebrating the faith that we have in the Lord Jesus. Anne LaMotte once said, "Laughter is carbonated holiness" (*Plan B: Further Thoughts on Faith* [New York: Riverhead Books, 2005], p. 66). Well said!

CHAPTER NINE

WIT, WISDOM, WRINKLES, AND WOWS

I am convinced that the Lord loves older people more and more. How can I tell? Because He is making more and more of us each day!

That is why it is crucial that we people of God get a grip on the emerging tsunami of mass aging that is taking place as we speak (or read). The world population, now at over seven billion people, experiences a net increase of nearly one million people over sixty every month. ("Demographic Profile of World Aging," www.un.org/news/DESA/United-Nations,1950-2050, accessed March 23, 2012.)

Now that is a lot of older adults!

The implications are obvious: a greater number of older adults means more challenges in health care, more caregivers needed, increasing medical costs, housing implications, financial concerns, ethical decisions, and on and on. However, with these challenges come many opportunities and blessings as well: more older adults to confess that Jesus is their Lord, more mentors for children and youth, more people of wisdom to share the story of Jesus and His love, more opportunities for generations to learn from one another, more stories to be told and life's legacies to be given, and on and on and on.

Psalm 78:4 reminds us "We will . . . tell to the coming generation the glorious deeds of the LORD, . . . and the wonders that He has done." What a great statement of faith about the role of all of God's people, especially older adults. The Lord equips us daily to be able to share this message of joy and forgiveness. As we share our faith with the next generation, it is also essential to note that they, too, are sharing their faith with us. People of all ages are enabled by the Spirit to share their faith stories.

So, where do we go from here? Let us first rehearse the four Ws of aging: wit, wisdom, wrinkles, and wow.

I remember hearing about a nurse in Portland, Maine, who was honored for her leadership in long-term-care nursing. She acknowledged this award by stating that she felt fortunate that her job gave her the three Ws: wit, wisdom, and wrinkles. Good answer, don't you think? I sensed from this that she certainly enjoyed her position, nurtured her sense of humor while serving others, shared her experiences by mentoring younger nurses, and celebrated growing older each day. What a great attitude toward life! What a great way to be in ministry every day with older adults as well as with people of all ages.

I personally added the fourth W: Wow! We have a built-in wow detector because we know we live on this side of the resurrection. As you and I use our wisdom to teach and train others, as we laugh at ourselves and help little kids and big kids do the same, as we celebrate the gift of aging in our own lives (wrinkles and all), we are also able to be intentional about sharing the "wow" of being loved and forgiven by God in Christ every day of our lives. The "wow" we share in the Lord is what makes life worthwhile. The wow of life is what makes the difference in the lives of others as we share our own wit, wisdom, and wrinkles, even in the midst of all of the woes around us.

Make sure you have a hearty laugh today. Laughter is like internal jogging, so the next time someone asks you if you jog, just say, "Yes, of course—I laugh." Share your wisdom with someone today also. Part of being wise is knowing when to share your wisdom and when just to listen. Be wise in your decisions. Certainly count your wrinkles, for they are the battle scars of a life well lived. I have a friend who does not appreciate wrinkles. As a matter of fact, she says that every time she goes to bed, she just lies there and can hear her skin wrinkling! Someone else told me that he thought wrinkles were only laugh lines, but then he looked at some people and decided that nothing could be that funny.

What kind of wows are popping up in and through your life? Watch for them. They are there. Name them! Tell others about them. If you sense that you are sometimes short of wows in your life, go out and look for them. Watch a little child at play; see that young person smiling and listening to her grandpa; watch the mom patiently wait for her child; see a father play catch with his son; look at a water bottle and remember your Baptism. Cross a street corner and make the sign of the cross on your chest to remind you of Christ's cross for us.

The Lord provides us with so many people around us, young and old, that we will never run out of finding and helping others to find the "wow" of life in the Lord. My encouragement right now is for each of us to become more aware of and more sensitive to older adults around us. Do not forget the younger ones, but instead, bring the older generations together with the young generations, and watch out for flying "wows."

We use our wit, share our wisdom, and celebrate our wrinkles, as we all grow gracefully in the "wow" of our Lord.

CHAPTER TEN

AGING GRACEFULLY: HOPE OR HYPE?

Little child:	"Ever been to a funeral?"
Friend:	"Sure, my grandpa's. My mom said he died of old age."
Little child:	"Yikes, I didn't know you could die from old age."
Friend:	"Be careful if you're around a lot of old people so you don't catch it!"

It seems safe to assume that since older adults are growing older and that there are more of us growing older longer, that more of us will be dealing with Alzheimer's and other physical issues, more of us will need a place where we will be cared for, and more of us will need caregivers and related services. And while we're at it, it's also safe to assume that there will be more of us with less money to pay for the care we need. To fantasize that aging is a beautiful thing and that everything will work out well can have grave consequences for our society—and the word *grave* has multiple meanings in this sense.

The question is, "Is aging gracefully hope or hype?"

To assume that each of us will grow older without medical, physical, and environmental issues is certainly hype, a myth. It is just not going to happen. That is what I have been trying to say through these pages: that growing old gracefully does not mean we will be ageless wonders and that pain and pills and problems will all disappear. To sugar-coat the aging process and try to convince people that cancer and arthritis and joint replacements and loneliness and financial concerns will bypass our door is not only wrong, it is foolish. In one sense, then, it is hype to encourage people to think that graceful aging does not include these realities.

On the other hand, as we realize more and more that life in the Lord is much more than dealing with worries, woes, and personal wars and instead recognize that life itself is a gift from God to be celebrated and shared, our vision of what aging is all about changes drastically. When we finally come to realize that our life is not something we earn or deserve or even own, this faith-filled fact changes our perception of life. With this realization, we look at life through the cross and resurrection instead of evaluating it by whether we are in good health, well-off financially, and have happy and caring people around us to take care of us.

Do you know someone who likes to ask, "Why me, Lord?" I do too. I even ask that question to myself on my "uh-oh" days. I need to remember, though, that it is much more healthy and honest and helpful to ask instead, "Why not me, Lord?" When I see that my life is a gift and not something I deserve, when I can admit that it is only by God's grace that I am living anyway, then I am arriving at the point in my life when I can see and say that yes, aging gracefully is all about hope in the Lord Jesus Christ.

This way of looking at life certainly does not resonate with everyone. For those people who do not see the Lord as the one who brings hope to the aging, I would agree that talking on and on about older people aging gracefully is probably seen as merely a word game. Aging gracefully is hype if we feel we deserve it and that life is ours to make what we want out of it. For example, take the sign that reads, "No Pain? Good!" Aging gracefully is hype if our goal in life is to get all we can out of it for our own satisfaction. Aging gracefully is hype if the Lord Jesus is not in the center of our lives!

Yes, as shown in the conversation between the two little kids above, there truly is an idea in our society that we had better be careful so we do not die of old age. Many people have died of old age, even at a very young chronological age, because they had given up on life, on themselves, and on the people around them. In my ministry years, I have met fifteen-year-olds who had already given up on life. I have also met some ninety-five-year-old people who have never caught the dreaded "old age disease," because they know and affirm that the Lord Jesus is alive and well in and through them. Let's pray that more people of every age will become immune to the hype of aging gracefully.

Let us also share the hope we have in the aging process because of Christ Jesus. Perhaps the Lord is allowing us to live longer so you and I have more time to share and tell the story of Jesus and His love. Let us bring the hope of aging gracefully to those who are still locked in to the hype of aging gracefully. We do this not by denying our pains and pills but by dealing with issues of life and death honestly and openly with others and by sharing our hopes and fears with others so they in turn can voice their hopes and fears with us. In the process, all the hype of aging gracefully can be transformed into the hope of aging gracefully, through the power of the One who brings us health and hope in Him. Now that is what life is all about in the Lord!

A few years ago, I developed a "myth list" on growing older. Check it out for yourself. (It's on the next page.) Discuss your thoughts on these myths with people younger and older than you. Listen to their views. Listen for any sign that to the people around you, aging gracefully is hype or hope. Have fun doing it!

The Myth List

- You can't teach an old dog new tricks.

- Thinking slows up as you age.

- All old people are wise.

- Old people want to be with people their own age most of the time.

- Old people can't keep track of family relationships and names.

- Old people want to be young.

- When you get old, you won't feel well.

- Intelligence declines with age.

- Aging people are past their prime.

- Old age is an illness.

- You won't live long if your parents didn't.

- Old people are more likely to become depressed.

- Old people are eccentric

- Old people stand little chance in a society that accents youth.

Aging gracefully: is it hype or hope? I'll take hope! How about you?

CHAPTER ELEVEN

THANK GOD I'M OLD!

Go ahead, say it out loud, or maybe just to yourself: "Thank God I'm old!"

There, that wasn't so bad, was it?

It can be difficult to thank God for our aches and pains and new wrinkles and having to visit the bathroom more often at night. However, at the same time, that does not take away from the fact that we are *able* to thank the Lord for this day as a new day to give away to others, starting with ourselves.

Our culture gives us permission to shout out, "Thank God I'm young," at least much of the time, but it is much tougher to gain acceptance from our society to affirm that being old is also a blessing. Just take a look at the birthday cards on the shelves at your favorite grocery store. Here we have, in living color (mainly black and gray), the strong message that birthdays, and therefore aging, is to be discouraged.

Here are a few of my favorites:

- A large elephant is on the front of the birthday card. Open it up and it reads: "Birthdays are Irr-elephant!" I disagree, Mr. Hallmark. Birthdays are *very* relevant, because birthdays mark another circle around the tree of our life. They proclaim that the Lord is not finished with us yet in this life.

- On the front is a picture of a birthday cake topped with hundreds of candles. Open it and it reads, "Please don't put a candle on your cake for each year of your life, because if you do, you'll burn the house down!" Wrong again, greeting card person. Instead, let us encourage people of all ages to light up the world with the joy and lightheartedness that is ours in Christ, the light of the world.

- A photo of an elderly person is on the front of the card, saying, "Ow!" Open the card and it reads, "Welcome to the 'random pains for no reason' years!"

- The quote on the cover reads, "I wouldn't call you old . . ." On the inside, it reads, "But if you were a car, you'd be a horse!"

- A picture of a lady on the front says, "You're having another birthday?" Inside, it states, "Aren't you old enough already?"

- Large-printed words boldly proclaim on the card: "We may be getting older," and on the inside it continues, "but psychologically and mentally we're as 'tarp as shacks!' "

- The front cover has a picture of a nice, yellow banana with one word below it: "Yesterday." Open the card, and on the inside is a picture of a spotted banana and the word: "Today." The caption reads, "Being one day older only matters if you're a banana!"

- And one more, which is a prime example of a mixed message using good humor: The front says, "Did you ever notice that the older you get, the younger you feel?" The punch line inside the card states, "Me neither!"

So what is the point of all of these cards and messages? Simply this: There is a very thin line in our society between laughing with older people and laughing at older people. Given the right attitude toward aging, some of the cards I've described here can be funny and appropriate to share with older adults. The point of our discussion is to discern what is the real message about aging in our society. Is it something to deny, laugh at, or forget it's happening? Or is it something to engage, encourage, and celebrate as a wonderful gift from God? I choose the latter!

CHAPTER TWELVE

THE THREE *R*s OF AGING

When we were in school, the three *R*s were *R*eading, '*R*iting, and '*R*ithmatic! However, let me suggest that in the process of aging gracefully, a different three *R*s are appropriate:

- Remembering
- Reframing
- Rejoicing

They are appropriate because of another *R*—the resurrection! Anyone who ages in the Lord is a resurrection resource. We live on this side of the resurrection, which empowers us to remember, reframe, and rejoice. The Scriptures are packed full of stories of how God reminds us of His faithfulness to us by engaging us in remembering, reframing, and rejoicing.

As I travel throughout the country, I regularly ask the older adults I speak to identify their concerns and worries about growing older. Here are the main concerns they articulate: health issues, having enough money, who will take care of me, how I will die, having friends, having a purpose or significance in life. I think that the most significant that surfaces is the feeling of insignificance.

What would you add to this list? As you think about answering that question, let's look at these concerns, keeping in mind the three Rs of aging: remembering, rejoicing, and reframing.

In terms of the fear of dying, notice that death itself is not the issue so much, but rather the fear of *how* they might die. I think it was Woody Allen, that quasi-theologian, who said, "I am not afraid of dying, I just don't want to be there when it happens!"

It is revealing (another *R* word) that according to this study, the biggest concern of older people is "feeling insignificant." The feeling of being insignificant is significant in itself. This feeling can prevent people from remembering the blessings of the Lord. It can block people from reframing their lives to see the Lord present with His promise, and it can destroy any kind of rejoicing in the Lord, because insignificance paints us as victims rather than as victors.

How significant or insignificant do you feel right now, and why? Does what you do or who you are impact your feelings of significance? A friend of mine recently retired as a CEO of a large firm. He was quite successful, but he eagerly looked forward to the day he would leave his position. However, after finally retiring, his happiness did not last long. After a few months of golfing, traveling, and just sitting around, he admitted that without his title as CEO, he felt less and less significant. He was the *former* CEO, which seemed to take away his worth and purpose in life.

Someone once said to me, "Rich, you sure have a promising future behind you!" Funny though it may be, it is not easy for some people to lose their position, their title, and therefore their perceived worth as a person, at least in the way society looks at success and significance.

We can learn much and be affirmed in the Lord by listening to the apostle Paul in the Scriptures. Isn't it amazing and revealing that Paul affirms that we are the people of God? He loves us and has called us as His own. Paul writes, "Put on then, as God's chosen ones, holy and beloved, compassionate hearts, kindness, humility, meekness, and patience, bearing with one another and, if one has a complaint against another, forgiving each other; as the Lord has forgiven you, so you also must forgive" (Colossians 3:12–13). This is where our significance comes from: God's unconditional love for us in Christ Jesus.

In other words, now we can see ourselves as nouns instead of as verbs. We are the people of God because of what Christ has already done for us. We are significant because of the sign of the cross on our chest and the water of Baptism on our forehead. Our significance has nothing to do with what we do (verbs) but rather has everything to do with whose we are (nouns). We are the people of God, and because we are nouns, we now serve Him by being verbs as we love and forgive and care for people around us.

Too often, people of all ages get it mixed up. We think we first have to act nice and look nice and feel nice to be a person of God. Not so, says the Lord! Our faith does not depend on how we act or on how we look or even on how we feel. Instead, our faith depends on the fact that Jesus Christ has lived, suffered, died and risen for you and me. Faith always receives God's love and forgiveness from the One who gives us significance. On the Crossings Community Web site, founder Edward Schroeder remarked that "faith is always in the catcher-position, receiving the Spirit-mediated pitches from God-in-Christ" (www .crossings.org/thursday/2011/thur102711.shtml [accessed December 22, 2011]). We are always on the receiving end of faith, and then we do something with what we've received, in the name of Jesus. It is all about us catchers receiving something that is coming from the mound (or mount!), where all Gospel gifts begin. So endeth this "Sermon on the Mound"!

Where does reframing fit in with the aging process? The gift of aging gives each of us an opportunity to reframe our lives. It allows us to come to grips with our impending death and to reach out to those around us in love and peace before we die. Reframing also allows us to work at prioritizing what is important in life. Have you made your "bucket list" yet? I affirm that activity as long as it does not become totally self-serving. Sure, it would be great if I could travel around the world and see all its wonders. However, perhaps some of my time and money could also be spent on feeding hungry people and befriending lonely ones, who are also God's wonders.

Perhaps I should delete "Making sure I have enough money to cover all my future needs and wants" from my bucket list and instead add, "Contributing at least 20 percent of my finances to support my favorite social ministry organizations." Perhaps I could reframe my future a little by adding, "Provide scholarships for ten children to continue their higher education" in place of "Plan to go skydiving by the time I am eighty." Come to think of it, I am feeling better about that last idea already.

Remembering who and whose we are and reframing our priorities in our daily lives automatically moves us to the third *R*: rejoicing. Rejoicing is an outcome of whose we are and what we do. Rejoicing enables us to see ourselves and others as both nouns and verbs by first seeing ourselves as nouns in the Lord.

Rejoicing is not our goal in life. It is the result of our life in the Lord, regardless of our age. Paul reminds us, "Rejoice in the Lord always; again I will say, rejoice" (Philippians 4:4). This reminds us not that all of life is one big bowl of cherries but rather that Christ's death and resurrection for us is what rejoicing is all about. Yes, pains and problems and pills will no doubt remain a part of our lives, but our joy in the Lord will never leave us—and that's His promise.

Enjoy living out the three *R*s of aging; well, really, four *R*s: remembering, reframing, and rejoicing, all because of the resurrection!

CHAPTER THIRTEEN

AMAZING GRAYS

"Amazing grace—how sweet the sound—That
saved a wretch like me! I once was lost but
now am found, Was blind but now I see!"
(*LSB* 744:1).

Look around you: there are so many "amazing grays" in
our lives who shout and share the fact that God's amazing
grace in Christ comes to us each and every day. There are
so many "amazing grays" who still have enormous energy
and enthusiasm and who are ready and eager to share with
others. The role of the Church is to put these senior saints
in ministry range of others and to provide opportunities
for them to share their hope-filled faith. I am reminded of
something Martin Luther probably did not say, but perhaps should have: "The only difference between a puddle
and a geyser is enthusiasm!"

Check this out for yourself. Think of older adults in
your family, congregation, community, or workplace who
smile and serve and celebrate their faith by what they say
and do and how they do it. Amazing, isn't it?

Confucius once said (although I did not hear him personally!), "It doesn't matter how slowly you go, as long as you do not stop." Now, it seems obvious that Confucius did not drive on too many expressways, but despite that, his point is well taken. We have been gifted by God to live each day as a day to praise Him and then give away to others! The point in living is to use our energies to share our faith and our experiences. Pastor Walt Schoedel often talks about there being three kinds of older adults: the go-gos, the slow-gos, and the no-gos.

The go-gos are those folks who are physically able to take trips, go to elder hostels, participate in mission trips, hop on a plane to visit the grandkids, and do many activities in their congregation and community. The slow-gos are able to attend some events, so they pick and choose which activities to participate in and when, depending on their energy levels. The no-gos are those who are homebound and not able to be about as much as they had been or as much as they'd like to be.

The key point here, however, is that *all* of these amazing grays are goers! They have not given up on life, even though their knees and other joints have given up on them. They may not be able to jog or participate in a touch-football game, but they are still willing and able to cheer others who do. They may miss attending evening church functions, but they accept the fact that their eyes are not strong enough to drive at night. They still participate with family and friends through prayer and phone calls and kind notes and inviting people over to visit with them.

Too often, it seems, individuals and congregations have a game plan that is desirable and ambitious. But the problem is that often these actions never materialize. Perhaps it is because their unofficial motto is: "Get ready, get set, get set, get set—but never go!" "Amazing grays" are people on the go.

"Amazing grays" are people of God who see aging as a blessing and not a burden, who find their new normal in life, and who adjust to various limitations and a different pace for their day. At the same time, they see themselves as people of God on the go even if they are not in the fast lane!

My friend Adolph is a great example of a no-go who is still going strong. At ninety-six, Adolph is writing a book, a history of his life and his ministry experiences in Addison, Illinois. Now, why should a person ninety-six years old endeavor to write a book? Well, why not? Although he is a no-go physically, he has a go-go mentality, and he wants to share his life in the Lord with those who come after him. Another exciting thing is happening through Adolph's project. People at the Lutheran Home are finding high-school volunteers to assist this budding author by typing his manuscript from his handwritten notes. This project is a great example that ministry happens not only by finishing a project but also along the way! Way to go, Adolph!

My friend Dick is another go-go kind of a guy. His hair is white, but he is truly an "amazing gray"! A few years ago, Dick asked a number of his friends to serve on his personal board of directors. What, we said? Now why would an eighty-year-old want to start a personal board of directors? "Simple," Dick responded, "because I need people around me to help me plan for my future!"

Just think of that: an eighty-year-old who has celebrated life in the Lord for so many years, still seeing and sensing the need for people around him to encourage and nudge and support him in his later years. As you can imagine, those of us on his personal board of directors are being blessed and guided as much as—if not more than—we are guiding him. That is what ministry is all about!

I encourage you to thank the Lord today for all of the "amazing grays" around you. If you are one of them yourself, thank the Lord for the gifts He keeps on giving you as you get ready, get set, and go, in the name of the Lord.

CHAPTER FOURTEEN

"Aha" Moments

Have you had an "aha" moment recently? Some experience that the Lord placed right in your lap without your planning it?

Sure you have, because you and I live on this side of the resurrection, which is the biggest and best "aha" moment of them all!

Sometimes, however, the "aha" moments around us get lost or obscured by the "uh-oh" moments that bombard us daily. It happens in our school, congregation, family, community, and throughout the world. It happens when you and I are not seeing and sensing the promise and love of the Lord working through our lives constantly.

But rejoice, "aha" people of God! The Lord has promised to be with us through our "uh-oh" days as well as our "aha" days. He promised that to us in our Baptism, which marks us for life as His "aha" people, regardless of how we look, act, or feel.

One way to celebrate and share our "aha" moments is to watch for these God sightings in all that we do. Use your six senses to focus and find experiences that the Lord provides for you every day. Notice that I said six senses and not five.

For too long, we have taught that we have five senses: sight, sound, touch, smell, and taste. Another extremely important sense we have as a gift from the Lord is our sense of humor. To realize this is an "aha" moment in itself!

I played with this sixth sense of humor on a recent plane flight. There I was, thirty thousand feet up, after a day of too many "uh-ohs" and too few "aha's." "Why not?" I thought. "Let's have some fun by thinking of possible 'aha' experiences that could happen to me as I 'fly the friendly skies.'" Here is what I hastily scribbled on my airplane "barf bag" (sorry, but there are few frills left on these airplanes):

"Aha" Moments: A View from Above:

1. There were fewer than four preschool children within screaming range of me.

2. I did not have to share a row with a sumo wrestler.

3. I was not sitting next to a cell phone junkie. By the way, I firmly believe that phone calls on airplanes should be limited to emergency situations only. I do not need to eavesdrop on people calling to say goodbye to their dog, someone calling his beloved to tell her that he is now sitting on the plane, or even someone using that great phrase, "Whatcha doin'?" The only conversation I am willing to listen to would be an emergency, such as, "Hello, this is Dr. Watson. Is the patient ready for her transplant?

Good, here are the steps to take until I arrive at the hospital."

4. I was not sitting next to someone who brought a picnic lunch with him, complete with pizza, tacos, greasy french fries, garlic, or other strong-smelling foods.

5. I fantasized that I would request that the flight attendant walk over to that one screaming kid in seat 23A and place him in the overhead compartment for the rest of the flight. (But, rejoice my friends; I did not do it!)

Another "aha" moment struck me as the flight attendant went through her drill prior to our takeoff. You know how it goes: "Everyone needs to be seated with his or her seat belt fastened and his or her seat backs in the upright, locked position. In case of an emergency [oh yeah, thanks!], an oxygen mask will drop from above. Place your oxygen mask on first, and then help those around you who may need assistance." Now that's a theological statement! Yes, we need to take care of ourselves first, in body, mind, and spirit, so that we are able to serve and assist those in need around us. An "aha" moment, indeed!

However, the best "aha" moment was yet to come. I was engrossed in reading a book, *Free of Charge: Giving and Forgiving in a Culture Stripped of Grace*, by Miroslav Volf.

As I was focusing on the need to forgive others around me, the young man next to me, who had been sipping his Starbucks coffee throughout the flight, reached down to grab something from his briefcase. In the process, he spilled his coffee all over the lap of the person sitting next to him— and that would be me. He quickly responded, "Oh, I'm so sorry!"

I must confess that my first response was more of an "uh-oh" than an "aha," but, as I gathered myself together and glanced at the title of the book I was reading, I did have enough presence of mind to respond by saying, "You are forgiven. It'll dry!" Later on during the trip, I did confess to him that to be honest, I'm not sure how I would have responded if I had not been reading a book on forgiveness. We even had a nice conversation after this experience.

"Aha" moments are all around us. They often sneak up on us. Watch for them, share them, write them down, make them happen to others, expect them, give them away, and give thanks for them. Be an "aha" moment yourself to someone every day.

Whether you are flying thirty thousand feet above the earth or you feel like you are fifteen thousand feet below, celebrate God's "aha" moments in and around you. Whether you are in the classroom, at the staff meeting, in the kitchen, or at a birthday party, witness your faith in Christ's grace and mercy to others as you interact with them today.

Whether you are struggling with those "uh-ohs" or flying high as an "aha" person of the Lord, stop and listen, with all of your senses, to the promise and presence of the Lord in your life, right here, right now.

Thanks for being an "aha" moment to me and to all those around you this day.

What else is there to say but "aha"!

CHAPTER FIFTEEN

THE *D* AND *A* OF AGING

What is the DNA—or the *D* and *A*—of aging in your family, in your congregation, or even in your own mind? What is it about aging that you celebrate, that you fear, that you question, that you wonder about?

Let me suggest that the following *D* and *A* topics are worthy of your continuing discussion and consideration. Seek out others to discuss these concept areas with you. Check local resources in your own community, such as hospitals, libraries, universities, churches, community centers, non-profit organizations, and older adult living facilities.

Numerous congregations are developing their own Web sites and resource centers to provide support, counsel, and resources for their members and community. Why not consider forming an ARC—Adult Resource Center—in your area to gather and capture the myriad information available for older adults so they can find it and discern what will be most helpful for them. The good news is that there is a lot of information out there. But the bad news is also that there is a lot of information out there. The key is to sort through all of the resources available and choose which ones work best for you and your congregation and community.

Here is a list of *D* and *A* topics of aging that I hope will prove helpful for you to explore further with your peers:

1. Defining Aging: Look at how people are defining the process of aging. Compare these thoughts with the Scriptures, and note the similarities and differences. I like the saying, "If you change the way you look at things, the things you look at change" (author unknown). This is so true of aging.

2. Denying Aging: What examples of denying aging do you see around you? How can you enable others to see aging as a gift instead?

3. Declaring Aging: To declare aging as a gift is to affirm life as a gift in the Lord. Help people to declare and celebrate aging wherever and however they can.

4. Demonstrating Aging: We demonstrate aging to be a gift every time we encourage older adults to be involved in ministries of care and concern for others. Help older adults understand that the Lord is not through with them yet.

5. Dedicating Aging: Celebrate the lives of older people through anniversaries, special accomplishments, and finding ways to honor them.

6. Demanding Aging: People who demand aging often forget that aging is not an accomplishment we earn but rather a gift that God gives. To demand that we live longer than the Lord provides is to mourn what might have been instead of celebrating what was.

7. Doing Aging: This one is easy! Continue to model and enable others to "do" aging by using your gifts each day, taking care of your body, mind, and spirit very intentionally, and helping others do the same.

8. Destroying Aging: People tend to destroy aging by not taking care of their bodies, by living only for themselves and not mentoring others around them, and by seeing aging as a burden instead of as a blessing.

9. Describing Aging: This is a much needed *D* and *A*! Verbalize to others that aging is a gift to be lived and given away rather than an ordeal to be bothered with. Help describe aging as the healthy relationship that the Lord provides between Him, you, and those around you. Describe it and live it well!

10. Delighting in Aging: Be lighthearted about aging. Accept your age right now, today! Celebrate it by sharing your time and hours with others, go jump rope (or at least think about it), and maybe even

get a new wrinkle pierced. We delight in aging by delighting in God's love and forgiveness of us in Christ Jesus.

Here are some additional ways to live out your *D* and *A* of aging. Think of them as healthy hints of "aha-ing":

Celebrate life in the Lord. Smile and laugh a lot. Be an ageless explorer. Relentlessly pursue your passion for life. Love to tell the story of Jesus and His love! Speak and act with hope. For better health, do a lot of walking—especially with the Lord. Spend time with those who are younger and older. Plan for your future. Be kind to animals, little children, and yourself. Accept aging as a gift. Tell others how much you love them. Hang around with friendly people. Eat healthy food. Worship the Lord regularly. Encourage, encourage, encourage. Catch people doing things right. Turn your "oh, no's" into "aha's." Be a champion for the elderly. See every day as a day to give away. Be ready to tell a story or a joke to someone every day. Pray daily, even for grouches. Forgive others, starting with yourself. Stop global whining. Do nothing, just for the fun of it. Be a carrier of hope. Speak and act on behalf of the lonely, the lost, and the least. Plan to leave a legacy of laughter. Be ready to live well, age well, and die well. Don't take yourself so seriously. Use the phone and e-mail a lot. Be a mentor. Remember your Baptism daily. Finally, practice using these kinds of words: "aha," "I love you," "hooray," "ta-da," "you may be right and I may be wrong," "forgive me," "I'm sorry," "great job," and even "oops."

Again I say, "Rejoice in the Lord always" (Philippians 4:4) as you live out your *D* and *A* of aging!

CHAPTER SIXTEEN

PREPARING FOR AGING

Six-year-old to grandma: "How old are you?"

Grandma: "I'm seventy-two."

Six-year-old: "Did you start counting at one?"

How are you preparing for aging? I've heard people say, "If I knew I was going to live so long, I would have taken better care of myself." How true, how true!

One way to approach the gift of aging is to affirm that every day is a gift to give away! See your age right now as the best possible age for you right now, because, of course, it is your only option! I am concerned about older adults who sometimes say that they'd rather be younger, when "things were better." "Remember the good old days" is the cry of some. Personally, I do remember some of my past days, and while some were great, I am glad others are over. Who was it that said, "It's hard to be nostalgic when you can't remember anything"? It was probably the same person who quipped, "Nostalgia isn't what it used to be!"

No doubt most of us could agree that "we have a great future behind us!" Meaning, of course, that we have accomplished much in life so far, that we have been blessed by God beyond our expectations, and that we are thankful for all the gifts and opportunities He has given us. If you are not sure of this, stop a moment, check to see if you are still breathing, and then thank God and go on living! Have you ever wondered if the Lord is through with you yet? Have you ever queried if you still have a mission and purpose in life? Again, check your breathing. If you are breathing and reading this, then the Lord still has exciting things in mind for you!

Maybe the following story will help us focus on life as we age.

> A man was sitting on the edge of the bed, observing his wife turning back and forth, looking at herself in the mirror. Since her birthday was not far off, he asked her what she'd like to have for her birthday. "I'd like to be six again," she replied, still looking in the mirror.

> On the morning of her birthday, he got up early, made her a nice big bowl of Lucky Charms, and then took her to Six Flags amusement park. What a day! He put her on every ride available—the Death Slide, the Wall of Fear, the Screaming Monster Roller Coaster—everything! Five hours later, they staggered out

of the theme park. Her head was reeling and her stomach felt upside down.

He then took her to McDonald's, where he ordered her a Happy Meal with extra fries and a chocolate shake. Then it was off to the movies, with popcorn, a big soft drink, and her favorite candy, M&M's. What a fabulous adventure! Finally, she wobbled home with her husband and collapsed into bed, exhausted. He leaned over his wife, and with a big smile, he asked, "Well, dear, what was it like being six again?" Her eyes slowly opened and her expression suddenly changed. "I meant my dress size, silly!"

We prepare for aging by living each day in the now. We prepare for aging by seeing and sensing the Lord at work in us right now. Many of us are so busy living each day that we do not take the time to think about aging—and that can be a good thing. I recall that as a young boy, I would cry every once in a while, evidently for no cause. No, my brother was not hitting me, nor had our dog, Spud, attacked me. I just started crying. I remember vividly that when my mom would ask, "Richie, why are you crying?" I would say, "I don't know," even though I did know. I was crying because I was afraid of dying. I was so worried about growing older and dying that I had forgotten how to live day by day.

On the other hand, young and middle-aged people have not had enough experiences in life to understand the whole process of aging. That is certainly not their own fault, but it is rather a given as we grow in years. To age well is to understand God's promise and God's presence in us. To age well is to have experienced the "uh-ohs" of life in order to be able to celebrate the "aha's" of life. I often hear the old saying, "Old age is not for sissies." That has some merit to it, but I would also contend that youth is not for sissies either! The Good News we share as God's people in Christ is that we all are sissies, afraid of life and afraid of death, but we are redeemed and forgiven in Christ Jesus!

The last stanza of the hymn "How Firm a Foundation" seems appropriate at this time: "Throughout all their life-time My people will prove My sov'reign, eternal, unchange-able love; And then, when gray hairs will their temples adorn, Like lambs they will still in My bosom be borne" (*LSB* 728:5).

We prepare for aging by living right now. When we be-come so obsessed with worrying about growing older, we lose the joy, awe, and wonder of the whole aging process. Let's face it: you and I are unable to prepare completely for aging, because we do not hold the future in our own hands. What we can do is to live every day in the best way possible, and that is to know that we are loved and forgiven in Jesus Christ. Holding on to that truth, we are able to launch out into our brave new world, not knowing where we are going exactly but knowing who is going with us.

If we become too distracted by wondering what our future holds, we miss the joy-filled opportunities of life right now today. Planning too intently for the future steals the gifts of this moment from us. Perhaps we can compare this situation to the dissection of a frog: you can dissect a frog very thoroughly, but, in the long run, it doesn't do you much good, nor is it that helpful to the frog!

To be quite honest, I am not sure that anyone can fully prepare for growing older, except by knowing that our future is secure in Christ! I do know that the pains, struggles, and roadblocks that come as we age, through dysfunction, disease, distress, desires, demands, and dumb actions on our part, all contribute to equipping us to age more gracefully and honestly. The hurts, hardships, and horrible happenings, which we all experience and which we will all continue to experience, woo us closer to the Lord rather than push us away from Him, as the Spirit leads and guides and upholds us in the faith. We age well, not because we are finally figuring out how to age well but because we see the Lord constantly at work in and through us, come thick or thin. Romans 5:2–5 says it best: "And we rejoice in hope of the glory of God. Not only that, but we rejoice in our sufferings, knowing that suffering produces endurance, and endurance produces character, and character produces hope, and hope does not put us to shame, because God's love has been poured into our hearts through the Holy Spirit who has been given to us." We age well, not only through the joys and positive moments of life but also through the worries, woes, and wars that we face. Moreover, the Lord is there through it all, showing us the way.

With the promise of God as a given, knowing that each day is a gift from Him, what are some simple things we can ponder and discuss about growing older? Try these on for size:

1. Thank the Lord daily for life itself. Thank the Lord for the open roads as well as the detours.

2. Remember our Baptism. It is always a given! We are redeemed in Christ!

3. Spend time with older people. Talk to them. Listen to them. Pick out some traits in them that you want to emulate. Learn from them.

4. Do not complain about your age to someone older than you.

5. Be intentional about living well and aging well so you can die well.

6. Talk to friends and family about your death and theirs.

7. Bring encouraging words to younger and older people every day. Be an encourager to all.

8. Look for trouble! As Zorba the Greek says, "Life is trouble. Only death is not. To be alive is to undo your belt and look for trouble." Actually, friend Zorba was close, but not really that helpful. Instead, I think he meant to say, "Look for the troubled: the lonely, the sick, the young, and the old, those who think God has forgotten them!"

9. Continue to "Easterize" people by sharing the story of Jesus' love in what you say and what you do.

10. Celebrate in grand style, with hoorays and alleluias, God's gift of aging, the "aha's" as well as the "uh-ohs," every day!

CHAPTER SEVENTEEN

Put Your Blinkers On

We experience the challenges of growing older. Notice that I did not call them the *woes* of growing older; however, there are indeed challenges as we mature in age. It is all about finding our new state of normal. It is all about accepting that things we once could do without thinking are now hard to remember, even with thinking. It is called aging, a gift from God!

I rejoice that I do not have to worry about remembering everything. I rejoice that perhaps my family and friends do not even expect me to remember a lot of my recent past. I rejoice that my mind can be less cluttered with all those things that are not all that important anyway. However, I must confess that it does bother me when I cannot remember the name of a friend, or where I put my glasses, or where I put my cell phone. Have you ever had to call your own cell phone and hope you can hear it so you can find it again? Me too!

I am also working at getting ready to forget more things, to slow down my pace, and to adjust to a quieter lifestyle. I know I will need help, and I will let others around me know that I need help. In other words, I need to learn to put my blinkers on!

I'm reminded of a true story of an eighty-year-old man who was having difficulty driving his car. When he would be out on the highway, he would be going so slow that other people would zoom by him, yell at him, make gestures at him, and generally show no respect for him. He would stay in the right-hand lane and try not to cut off anyone; he just wanted to reach his destination safely. (Perhaps he might have his left-turn signal on, but that is another story!)

This elderly gentleman confessed to his son that he was getting more and more frustrated when people were rude to him on the roads. His son listened for a while and then suggested this strategy: "Dad," he said, "when you are driving on the highway, why don't you just leave your hazard lights blinking so people know you are moving slowly?" "Good idea," the elderly man said. "I'll give it a try." A few days later, the older man confessed to his son, "You were right! The hazard light works great! As a matter of fact, some people slow down just to see if I am okay. Others roll down their window and ask if they can help me with something. It's amazing how people do not see me as a confused old man anymore but as someone who might need their help!"

The moral of the story for us older adults: Put your blinkers on!

Let others know that you need help. Ask for assistance. How can people around us know that we need something if we do not tell them? This behavior is difficult for people who do not want to admit that they need help. If you are too proud to ask for help, you are still going to get judged and hassled and receive dirty looks and gestures. The risk is that you will stop living and be so concerned about not doing something right or well that you do not even try anymore. It is up to us. Personally, I think I'll put my blinkers on.

This reminds me of a time I went to a large bookstore to buy a book. I was becoming frustrated because of the rows and rows of books, and I could not find the correct section. So, I decided to ask for help. I went up to a charming-looking "bookster" and said, "Excuse me, could you help me find the self-help section of books? She looked at me with a quizzical gaze and replied, "Sir, if I told you, it would be defeating the purpose, wouldn't it?"

Despite the previous anecdote, I strongly encourage us older people to ask for help. Most of the time, other people are willing and able, and sometimes even eager, to help us. People have actually held the door for me as I entered a store. One nice young man even said, "There you go, sir," when he helped me find my cell phone I had misplaced. And of course we've all heard the story about the Boy Scout who took a little old lady's arm to help her through a busy intersection—but she didn't want to cross the street!

As we age, we need to practice being vulnerable. We

need to loosen up on our pride and see that the Lord is putting people around us all the time because as we age, we need more and more help with various tasks. Letting others help us is not a burden to them. We can help other people feel good about themselves by letting them help us. It is not becoming weak, it is not that we are failures; rather, it is our new state of normal and a great opportunity and ministry that we can provide for others. If we can assist that Boy Scout in getting his merit badge in the process, all well and good!

Put your blinkers on! You are a gift to others!

CHAPTER EIGHTEEN

KEEPING OUR AGING BODIES WELL

> "Exercise kills germs, but how do you get
> them to exercise?"

(Author unknown)

It is a known fact that our aging bodies need regular exercise. Study after study shows the health value of a regular routine of keeping our bodies moving, stretching, and active. For example, the World Health Organization recommends that most people get 150 minutes a week of moderate aerobic exercise and strength training (World Health Organization, "Physical Activity and Adults," http://www .who.int/dietphysicalactivity/factsheet_adults/en/index .html [accessed December 23, 2011].) Another study points out that exercise relieves migraine headaches. Still another finding is that older adults who exercised for fifteen minutes a day (or an average of ninety-two minutes per week) extended their lifespan by three years compared to people who were inactive. A person's risk of death from any cause decreased by 4 percent for every additional fifteen minutes of exercise per day.

It is also worth noting that people who are retired reported that their lives are either the same (44 percent) or better (29 percent) than during the five years before they retired. Many say they experience less stress, and most say their relationships are better, they eat better, and they spend more time doing things they enjoy, such as exercise and other activities.. However, 25 percent of new retirees say their life is worse. ("Retires and Those Near Retirement Have Different Views of Golden Years," http://www.hsph .harvard.edu/news/press-releases/2011-releases/retire- ment-poll.html, accessed March 23, 2012.)

The majority of people surveyed say they expect to live past 80 (78 percent of pre-retirees, 72 percent of retirees). An optimistic group of retirees (32 percent) expect to live at least to ninety, whereas a lesser amount (29 percent) of pre-retirees think they will hit that magical age. By the way, it has also been shown that the older you are, the healthier you were!

Whether people are working full-time or part-time, most agree that to take care of their health, they need to focus on maintaining good relationships with friends and family, watch their weight, and see a doctor regularly.

Studies and surveys such as those mentioned above are indeed helpful for us to get a sense of how we can develop and keep healthy habits of living well. We need the support and ideas of others to encourage and sustain our endeavor to keep well in body, mind, and spirit. However, as the people of God, we need to consider a number of other factors in our search for health and wellness for ourselves. First, why do we want to keep healthy in the first place? Also, what other factors play into our living well in the Lord as we live each day to honor Him and to serve others?

Martin Luther had much to say about the importance of taking care of our own bodies. He emphasized that people of God take care of themselves in order to be able to care for and serve their neighbors. Certainly, it is important for us to work at keeping our bodies healthy so we feel better and so we do not need to become dependent on the many pain relievers that are available. Naturally, we want to be well so we can travel and play with our grandkids and enjoy a quality life. And for Chicago Cubs fans, we want to remain healthy long enough so we can transport our aging bodies to Wrigley Field for a World Series not too many more years from now!

As God's people, we are motivated to take care of our aging bodies so we can live life to the full as we go about serving others to the full! A healthy body is not an end in itself; it is a means whereby we as God's gifts care for and love other people, all in the name of the healing Christ!

Therefore, we encourage ourselves and others to exercise regularly, watch what we eat, take time to rest, and manage our schedules. However, we do all these healthy habits not only to keep our weight down or energy levels up but also so we can serve others in the Lord! To say it another way, it is crucial that we take care of ourselves so we are able to take care of others. I am reminded of the flight attendants on airplanes who always remind us before each flight: "Put your oxygen mask on first, and then assist others who need help with their oxygen masks!" What a great reminder for our life in the Lord! The Spirit breathes life into us each day, in body, mind, and spirit, so we can be healthy holy witnesses to people around us who are in need of the Spirit's breath as well!

I recently overheard a discussion between a father and his son. His son evidently was a late sleeper, because his dad was urging him to be more active and to rise earlier in the morning. "But Dad, don't you realize that sleeping is a very important part of keeping healthy, and that people sleep at least one-third of their lives?" "Yes, I agree," the father responded, "but in your case, you're only sixteen years old so you've already slept for more than five years!"

The point is to practice health habits of living and take good care of yourself for the right reason: to celebrate life as a gift from God by giving your life to others!

CHAPTER NINETEEN

LOOKING FOR HOPE IN ALL THE RIGHT PLACES

"Hope is knowing that even when there is no hope, there is hope in Jesus Christ!"

(Author unknown)

I like this definition of hope. It is energizing, revealing, affirming, true, and of course, hopeful! Hope is another one of those gifts that God has given to us, especially to us older people. We have lived through hopeless and hope-filled times. We have experienced hope fasts and hope feasts. We have struggled when we have put our hope in something other than Jesus Christ and His righteousness.

I contend that one of the challenges in our Church, school, and society is that there are not enough hope peddlers around. It is tough, to say the least, to be hope-filled Easter people in a Good Friday world. Churches and communities and countries and even families often have the wrong enemies. We "shoot the wounded." Too often, we say no to people when what they need is a reassuring yes in the Lord. Too often, we misread and misquote Luke 10:2, "The harvest is plentiful, but the laborers are few." Instead, our lives seem to indicate that it reads, "The harvest is plentiful, but the workers are arguing."

Perhaps we are being led to look for hope in all the wrong places: in the daily news instead of in the Good News; through the latest reality TV show (which, in reality, is not really reality); through the philosophy of a prosperity gospel instead of the Gospel of the cross and resurrection; through a belief system that espouses "Let go and let God," instead of a faith life that affirms that God in Christ already has a firm grip on us. The examples go on and on.

Where do you find hope? Or, more precisely, in whom do you find hope? Who finds hope in you? One hopeful sign in all of these questions is that we as God's people, the "holy huddle of hope" people, are gifted through Christ Jesus to be signs and hands and voices and hugs of hope in the world, as we begin each day in our Baptism. We are called out as God's hope-filled people to enable others to find hope in all the right places!

A hope-filled friend of mine, Bob Sitze, puts forth the following truths about hope:

- Hope is rooted in the many manifestations of spirituality throughout history.

- Hope is based emotionally and rationally on faith.

- Hope is best discovered, felt, known, practiced, strengthened, habituated, and internalized within human relationships.

- Hope does not manifest itself only in niceness or positive feelings.

- Hope works best as a disciplined habit that can counteract addictions to fear, anger, and despair.

Well said, hope-filled Bob! (Check out Bob's latest book, *It's Not Too Late: A Field Guide to Hope* [Herndon, Virginia: The Alban Institute, 2010].)

How can we be hope leaders in this hopeless world? Mull over these suggestions as you consider other possibilities in your own life:

1. Use hope-filled words intentionally. Do an audit of your spoken and written communications.

2. Ask loved ones around you to critique your words and your actions. Do they look in the right places for hope from you?

3. Pick one arena of your life—your home, congregation, school, or workplace—to say and do hope to others. How does it feel? What reactions do you receive?

4. Look in the mirror or ask a friend to check your facial expressions and body language. Humans copy what they see in others.

5. Evaluate what and who makes you angry. Analyze your feelings, ask help from others, and reinvent ways to respond to others in hope.

6. Spend more time with hope-filled people. Our hope levels need to be restored regularly.

7. Search the Scriptures. In them is real hope! Do a concordance study of all the hope passages; it's an amazing experience!

8. Tell others of "the hope that is in you" (1 Peter 3:15).

9. Keep well in body, mind, and spirit by looking for hope in all the right places: in Word and Sacrament; in the body of believers, the Church; in Baptism.

10. Know that there still is hope in Jesus Christ! Our faith and hope in Christ do not depend on how we look, act, or feel, and that's a good thing. It all depends on what Christ has already done for us on the cross and in the resurrection.

Vibrant Faith Ministries, an exciting ministry organization in Minneapolis, shares some of the following thoughts in terms of what we hope-filled people of God are being called to do in today's world:

- Get over it: the 1950s (and '60s and '70s) are over. We are living in a new time.

- It is difficult doing ministry during these times, but it always has been difficult.

- Now is the perfect time for Christians to innovate, adapt, and experiment in a ministry of hope.

- All innovation will take place through the power of the Holy Spirit.

- Most significantly, Jesus is the Lord of hope in all centuries and in all places.

(Adapted from Paul Hill, "Welcome to the 1st Century . . . Again." Vibrant Faith Ministries. http://www.youthandfamilyinstitute.org/thoughtsfrompaul.html [accessed January 4, 2012].)

My hope-filled prayer is that we people of hope will rub ministry shoulders with one another to encourage, build up, affirm, embrace, smile, laugh, and forgive as we move out into this often hopeless world to bring health and hope to all people, starting right now with the people in front of us.

Paul wrote, "May the God of hope fill you with all joy and peace in believing, so that by the power of the Holy Spirit you may abound in hope" (Romans 15:13).

Now that is what I call looking for hope in all the right places! Okay, older adults, what are we waiting for?

(This chapter appeared as "Multiplying Ministries: Looking for Hope in All the Right Places," by Rich Bimler. *Lutheran Education Journal*, March 21, 2011. http://lej.cuchicago.edu/columns/multiplying-ministries-looking-for-hope-in-all-the-right-places/ [accessed January 4, 2012]. Reprinted by permission.)

CHAPTER TWENTY

THE REAL WORLD HEALTH ORGANIZATION

"The Church is like mountain climbers: the
reason mountain climbers are tied together
is to keep the sane ones from going home!"

(Author unknown)

The World Health Organization, headquartered in
Geneva, Switzerland, is a marvelous gift to the world. For
years, this committed group of people has studied global
health needs, provided excellent information, continued
significant research and development efforts, trained mil-
lions of people in health awareness, shared resources galore, and served as a conscience for people and other health
organizations to take health and wellness seriously on this
planet.

With all this said, we also strongly need to point out
that the *real* World Health Organization is not in Geneva,
Switzerland. No, the real World Health Organization is
your congregation, the Church, the Body of Jesus Christ!

Through Word and Sacrament and demonstrating
God's love for all people in Jesus Christ, your congrega-

tion and mine are the primary givers of health and wellness to people young and old throughout the world, all in the name of the healing Christ.

How often we forget this! Too often, we get so caught up in emphasizing the fact that the Church is indeed the gathering place of God's people that we fail to emphasize that Christ's Church is also the scattering place of health and hope to the world. Now, by this we do not mean that the congregation should forget about sharing the message of Jesus Christ or fail to teach God's Word as truth through the Scriptures. The very point is this: our congregation takes God's Word very seriously, and we know through faith that Jesus Christ is the Lord and Savior of the world. That is the very reason the congregation is the World Health Organization, because only through Christ is the world redeemed and made well! Consider the history of the Lutheran Church, for example. It is amazing how the Lord has used Lutherans to establish hospitals and homes for older adults throughout the world in order to care for those in need, as we proclaimed the Gospel loudly and clearly. We see ourselves as the World Health Organization, not because we have forgotten the Gospel of Christ but because we have remembered the Gospel of Christ.

I included the quote at the beginning of this chapter because it intrigues me. Your congregation and my congregation are bands of people who gather around water and

Word and bread and wine—common, ordinary things—to do extraordinary ministries because we have an extraordinary God! To the world out there, it seems insane, doesn't it? Why in the world do people gather around Word and Sacrament, spending precious time together (even during football season!) to celebrate and proclaim the hope that is within us? We gather together, knowing that no one is an island alone in this vast ocean of life, because we are all connected by the water of our Baptism. We are tied together in Christ, and we strongly and courageously sing, "Blest be the tie that binds Our hearts in Christian love; The fellowship of kindred minds Is like to that above. . . . We share our mutual woes, Our mutual burdens bear, And often for each other flows The sympathizing tear" (*LSB* 649:1, 3). Now, that is what the real World Health Organization is all about.

This discussion will lead us right into looking at congregations as the place where older adults as well as people of all ages can gather around the cross and the empty tomb. There, we build up one another in the faith in order for all of us to be equipped for ministry as God's healing agents, wherever we are. The Church, your congregation and mine, is the gathering place of the faithful, the holy huddle, the grace place, the shalom zone, the friendly flock. This is the place where the Lord in His marvelous ways brings His grace and hope and peace to us, and then He sends us out to rub ministry shoulders with others. Insane? Maybe to the world, but to us, God says, "You are a chosen race, a royal priesthood, a holy nation, a people for His own possession, that you may proclaim the excellencies of Him who called you out of darkness into His marvelous light" (1 Peter 2:9).

Keep us tied together, Lord, for we have a lot of healing to do!

CHAPTER TWENTY-ONE

THE AGING-FRIENDLY CHURCH

"Where is my Sunday paper?" the irate customer demanded, calling the newspaper office. "Ma'am," said the newspaper employee, "today is Saturday. The Sunday paper is not delivered until tomorrow, on Sunday." There was a long pause at the other end of the line, followed by a gasp of recognition as the customer muttered, "Well, shoot! So that's why no one was at church today."

"Church," your congregation, is a place where people can come, regardless of what day it is, to be renewed, refreshed, given hope, and forgiven in the name of Jesus. The Church is the place where Christ's forgiveness is for giving. Even when we forget what day it is or fail to forgive others or get caught up in ourselves, the Church is the place where hope abounds, where forgiveness restores, and where people are connected for mission and ministry in the world. We know that the Church is not about you or me; it is about Him! For that, we are thankful.

We also need to affirm that the Church is one of the few places where people of all ages come to do things together in the Lord. Yes, the family is still in place and it is still a key ingredient, although a recent statistic claims that the average parent spends 38.5 minutes per week in conversation with his or her children. (www.dinnertrade.com, accessed March 16, 2012.) But that is a topic for another book.

How is your congregation doing in terms of being friendly to people of all ages? What are some indicators that show how effective your congregation is in bringing older people and little kids together for sharing and developing faith? It is crucial that congregations take seriously their calling to bring people together around Word and Sacrament in intentional ways, equipping God's people to relate and rejoice with others in the faith.

The place to start in evaluating your congregation is to affirm that the best intergenerational ministry happens every time your parish comes together for worship. "Where two or three are gathered in My name, there am I among them" (Matthew 18:20). How thrilling it is to see people of all ages regularly celebrating their faith in the Lord! Too often, when we think of how and where older adults are involved in our congregation, we fail to affirm where all ministry to all ages begins: at worship every week, in the name of the Lord.

From the altar and the font, we can then move to other aspects of older adult ministry. We see older adults involved in weekly services through ushering, assisting in Communion, and in reading Scripture lessons. Perhaps they have other volunteer roles through your worship committee or in counting the offering. I observe at this point that older adults can and should be involved in these functions, but make sure that young people are also involved in similar ways. The best older adult ministries in congregations happen when people of all ages worship together, serve together, celebrate together, and are together in the name of the Lord.

There's nothing wrong with having an adult choir, but why not include young people as well? What a great opportunity for us older folks to be models and examples for the young. We might even learn how to talk and listen better to young people in the process.

Does your congregation have children's messages during worship? I certainly support them! I realize that ideally every part of worship is to unite people of all ages and direct them toward Christ, but I also recognize the benefits of being intentional about using language and styles that enable different ages of people to understand and connect more effectively. If you provide children's messages, why not also provide older adult messages? I can just hear the pastor say, "Okay, all you eighty-year-olds and up, come on down for the older adult message. You can lie down here; we'll help you up later!" Of course, I am being facetious, but I hope my point is clear. Let me say it again: aging-friendly churches provide ministry opportunities for people of all ages, both to individuals of every age as well as to every generation, individually and collectively.

Sermons can also be age-friendly when the pastor connects together the Scriptures and faith for all ages. This happens when positive illustrations concerning older adults are used with the Good News as well as with the daily news. This happens when the pastor acknowledges the touch points in the lives of people, such as couples celebrating fiftieth wedding anniversaries, older adults who have been recognized for significant honors, or those who just celebrated one hundred years of life. In general, sermons are age-friendly whenever aging is affirmed as a gift and blessing from the Lord rather than portrayed as a burden to handle.

Here are some other simple ways that congregations can and do emphasize that they are indeed age-friendly churches:

1. Provide opportunities for people of all ages to gather together for worship, service, fellowship, learning, and witness. I especially enjoy the potluck suppers that are great celebrations because they bring grandpas and little kids and single young adults together for one purpose: to celebrate life in the Lord (well, maybe for two purposes, because the food is always quite tasty!).

2. Enlist older adults as sponsors or mentors of confirmands every year. Ask older adults to keep a close connection with a newly confirmed person, pray for them, meet with them, send them birthday cards, and be a friend to them.

3. Ask older adults to be Baptism buddies for all newly baptized infants, children or adults, not to take away the role of godparents but rather to link an older person to a new believer in order that faith-stories can be shared regularly and intentionally.

4. Provide a place for older adults to meet regularly with their peers for monthly gatherings, lunches, speakers, events, and activities. This is no doubt the main activity of most churches in older adult ministries, and it is a very important one, but it is not to be seen as the only way that older adult ministry is done. It is merely one way, because there are many ways to tell the story of Jesus, who is the one way!

5. Develop an older adult advisory group to be responsible for making the congregation aware of older adult needs, planning events, and getting feedback about what gifts can be used and what needs can be met through older adult ministries.

6. Develop an ARC—Adult Resource Center—that encourages and assists older adults in finding needed resources in the community.

7. Organize community events to bring non-churched older adults into your faith community.

8. Take a survey of your community to ascertain what other needs are waiting to be met in your area. Is there a need for an older adult day-care center? Do older adults need transportation assistance? Can older adults team together to do volunteer service in the school and community? Can seniors volunteer their time for a relief agency or children's home? Can younger older adults regularly visit older adults in a local Lutheran Home facility? And so on.

9. Provide courses to enable adult children to understand and communicate better with their aging parents. Offer Bible classes for people of any age. Encourage older adults to volunteer to teach and assist in Sunday School classes and Vacation Bible School. While you are at it, why not sponsor an adult VBS for older adults? Don't forget the snow cones!

10. Invite older adults from neighboring congregations to join your older adult group for a trip, a retreat, a mission project, or just a good time together, and talk about the good old days!

11. Be intentional about publicly celebrating important milestones in the lives of your older members: birthdays, anniversaries, moving from one place to another, retirement, birth of grandkids and great-grandkids, or even the renewal of a driver's license. Be creative!

12. Ask questions. Who is responsible for older adult ministries in your congregation? If the answer is "no one," advocate for someone to be designated as the point person for older adult ministry. It can be a staff person, a volunteer, a young person, an older person, but make sure it is someone who can advocate for the older adult ministries. Let him or her be a "divine irritant" to help your congregation be more aware of and pro-active in developing ministries for, with, of, and to older adults in your congregation and community.

This is just the start of powerful possibilities that await you and your congregation as you become excited and involved with older adults. Why not get a few other folks together to dream of more ways for older adults to be a strong, positive ministry force in your congregation? We've only just begun!

One more suggestion: If at any time you hear someone in your parish complaining that there seem to be more and more blue-haired, white-haired, or no-haired people in worship and fewer young people and families, simply say, in an affirming way, "Of course, we want younger people and little kids and families to come to worship and be involved in our congregation, but if we do not have more blue-haired, white-haired, and no-haired people in our pews, we are not keeping up with the demographics of our community. There continues to be a greater number of older adults around, so there had better be older adults around us in worship. Praise the Lord!"

Amen to that!

CHAPTER TWENTY-TWO

MATTERING AND MENTORING

"I like to talk and be with my grandpa. He doesn't own me like my parents do!" From the mouth of a six-year-old!

Everyone wants to feel that he or she matters in life. Mentoring is one significant way to help people feel like they matter. Poet T. S. Eliot claimed that two of the greatest purposes in life were being important to others and making a difference in others' lives.

Who matters to you? To whom do you matter?

Who is your mentor? Whom are you mentoring?

These are powerful questions for people of every age, especially older adults.

Since I am name-dropping, it was Plato who said, a long time ago, that "what is honored in a country will be cultivated there." We can add that this is also true about church bodies, congregations, classrooms, and families. It is high time that we as God's messengers recapture the importance of putting people back within ministry range of each other, rather than pitting people against each other. We can tear down barriers and learn from one another through mentoring opportunities that make people matter to one another.

Andrea Dixon, in a 2007 issue of *Adultspan Journal*, lists five components of "interpersonal mattering":

1. Acknowledge my significance and value.

2. Interest.

3. Attention.

4. Trust.

5. Regard for my future wellbeing.

(Adapted from Andrea L. Dixon, "Mattering in Later Years: Older Adults' Experiences of Mattering to Others, Purpose in Life, Depression, and Wellness." *Adultspan Journal*, September 2007, http://www.highbeam.com/doc/1G1-170113346.html [accessed December 20, 2011].)

A major thrust of our culture that is working against us is the concept called CPA, or "continuous partial attention." Through iPods, smartphones, texting, and e-mails, we are pulled away from personally interacting with other people, all in the name of staying constantly connected with people. A recent comic strip shows a teenager in her bedroom, texting her parents in the kitchen to ask them when dinner will be ready. Sound familiar? Again, it was our friend T. S. Eliot who wisely remarked that we are "distracted from distraction by distraction" ("Burnt Norton," *Four Quartets* [San Diego: Harcourt, Inc., 1943, 1971], 1.3.101).

So, what are we going to do about it? For starters, how about committing ourselves to developing the art of mattering to each other? How about going out of our way to make intentional personal connections every day with at least a few people who matter to us as well as to those who also need to feel like they matter? Encourage each other to listen, really listen, to the little kids around us, as well as to the "amazing grays" in our lives. Mattering is not an easy assignment, at least for me. Mignon McLaughlin, the American journalist, once said that "no one really listens to anyone else, and if you try it for a while, you'll see why!"

Mentoring happens when we intentionally make eye-to-eye and heart-to-heart connections with someone else. We get to choose who mentors us, which is another great way to let people know they matter so much to us that we want to learn and grow with them. In a real sense, mentoring becomes a way to say, "You matter to me!"

What is the matter with all of these words written so far? Just this: Our relationships with others, as mentors and matterers, do not begin with us. Our connection with others has already begun through the life, death, and resurrection of the One who came to us to make things matter. Our Baptism connects each of us with Him as well as with everyone else, whether or not we listen or mentor—and that is a matter of fact.

Yes, the fact of the matter, Christ's love for us, does not get us off the hook to connect with others; rather, it empowers us to be a mentor and matterer to those around us. It is not that we "got to" matter to others, it's that we "get to" matter to others, because of Christ Jesus!

Let us go around not just trying to make it through another day but, more important, trying to matter to other people, always inspired and motivated by the love and forgiveness of Jesus Christ. Our Lord says to us right now, today, "I am the way, and the truth, and the life" (John 14:6).

That is really all that matters, and now we "get to" matter to others as well!

(This chapter appeared as "Multiplying Ministries. . . Mattering and Mentoring," by Rich Bimler. *Lutheran Education Journal*, June 14, 2010. http://lej.cuchicago.edu/columns/mattering-and-mentoring [accessed December 20, 2011]. Reprinted by permission.)

CHAPTER TWENTY-THREE

OUR CHANGING ROLE
AS WE GROW OLDER

Yes, we all continue to age, and that is a good thing. Relationships change, priorities change, friends come and go, and families move away. Perhaps we change so much that we come full circle and start repeating ourselves again and again. (Did I say that we even repeat ourselves?)

The Lord knew what He was doing when He made parents and grandparents to be the age they generally are. There is no way I could function as the father of a six-year-old at age 72. The aging process allows everyone to develop his or her God-given gifts and to use them in different ways at different times throughout their years.

In part, the aging process enables us to change to fit the environment in which we live. My role as a husband and father changes to adapt to the needs, gifts, and situations that surround me. There is no one way to be a good father or mother or grandpa or grandma. It depends on the "holy huddle" gathered around us. It depends on how I have used—and misused—my gifts and situations. It depends on how I am blessed with the gifts and love and forgiveness of those gathered around me.

Our roles in our family, workplace, congregation, and community certainly change drastically as well. At times, I catch myself seeing my grown children as if they were still little kids and, worse than that, treating them as such. I still picture my grandkids, who are now in their twenties, the same way I viewed them when they were much younger. When I fail to change how I view and treat people around me, I have failed to see how my role and relationship with them have changed. When that happens, communications break down, frustration is created, and expectations soar off the charts.

What different roles can you identify in your own changing life? How have relationships changed, grown, weakened, and stretched with the people close to you? Some of the most significant steps in the aging process are to learn to identify these changes, adjust your behavioral patterns, and talk through these changes with those around you. As we become better able to understand our changing roles, we can also help, encourage, and assist others around us to adjust to their aging children, neighbors, grandkids, and spouse.

I did a quick survey of our seven grandchildren, aged nine through twenty-two, to get a glimpse of how they perceive older adults in their family and community. Interesting indeed! Among other findings, I learned:

1. They like older adults and wish they could spend more time with them.

2. They want older adults to treat them as intelligent people.

3. They think that the young and the old need to communicate more about personal issues and "just to be there to talk to each other."

4. As they grow older, grandchildren want to participate in grown-up activities with older adults.

5. They want to hear about the past, but not "all the time."

6. They want older adults to be able to change their perceptions of younger people to be more positive. In their words: "Try not to be judgmental of how we look or act sometimes."

7. They want older adults to be willing to do what young people want to do, even if that means changing schedules and priorities. ("We really do like being with you!")

8. Tell them stories, but do not make them too long!

9. Help them better understand their parents. Be a translator!

10. They want to hear about older persons' faith and feelings.

Aging adults are continually in need of help to change behaviors, perceptions, and actions toward people older and younger than themselves. We can change only by being aware of the changing relationships around us and being willing to be assisted by those who can help us adjust and readjust to life's changing landscape. Who in your life is enabling you to make some necessary changes in your relationships? If no one comes to mind, consider who may be of help and support to you as we all make adjustments in our own lives and in how we relate to those around us.

Here are some possible responsibilities and changing roles you may have experienced or are experiencing at the present time:

1. Be a keeper of the history of your household. Keep telling the stories and connecting today's life with yesterday's experiences. Keep traditions alive. Keep touch points centered and visible. Celebrate each day as a family.

2. Be a translator between generations. Help the parents of your grandkids (those are your children, by the way!) better understand and listen to their children.

3. Be a listener and not so much a teller, as you possibly have been in the past.

4. Counsel and support family members and others by sharing ideas, concerns, and experiences with those younger than you.

5. Play more of a behind-the-scenes role in your family and community. Stay involved, but not necessarily as the leader or director. Be the quiet influencer that every home, congregation, and community needs.

6. Be an "Energizer Bunny." As much as possible, depending on your energy level, be the cheerleader, the enthusiast, that "way to go" person who encourages others on their path in life. One of our granddaughter's tumbling coaches, Steve, exemplifies this attitude. At sixty-eight years old, Steve coaches tumbling, gymnastics, and other aerobic sports. He says it this way: "I'm really not a coach; I am an encourager. I do not teach my students how to tumble; I teach them to believe in themselves so they use the gifts the Lord has given them. I teach encouragement." Well said, Coach Steve!

7. Be a financial advisor. Well, someone has to do it! If you have the gifts and expertise, the need for a sound financial voice in the family and community is critical. This role may change as children age, as parents age, and as the congregation ages. If you do not see yourself in this role, find someone to be this fiduciary friend.

8. Be a divine irritant. Sure, you can do it. This is someone who plays the role of a conscience sensor. Older

adults can be great questioners, not saying no all the time but rather raising the tough questions, helping others to share their thoughts and ideas, and keeping the family and community honest in their assessment of situations.

9. Help make others look good. This is a fun task! No need for older folks to be the champions of all the card games; no need to stomp over the ten-year-olds in a competitive game of chess. No need always to win the family's annual ten-yard dash. Stay competitive, but help others also feel good about team sports and competition. This has not been a problem for me recently because I do not even have to try to lose anymore. The kids and grandkids whip me in just about everything except the "who goes to bed the earliest" contest.

10. See yourself as not only serving as the head of the house, if that indeed is or was the case, but also more and more as the heart of the home. Be a person who is available for others, someone who is always there. Be the person who has the time to play with and color with and read to the younger ones. Be the taxi cab driver, the grocery store runner, the "oops, Hannah forgot her lunch" person, and even the person who offers to take care of the dog some weekends.

A great joy in growing older is having opportunities to care for others in small ways. There is a certain relief in realizing that you no longer need to be the center of the family—if indeed you ever were. There is a quiet realization that the family and neighborhood and congregation might just be able to get along without you after the Lord calls you home. There is a sense of joy and peace in knowing that the Lord has certainly blessed others through you and that He can also give those blessings through others who will and can take your place. Our changing roles in life, in our families and in other places, can bring about that peaceful moment when once again we hear the Lord say, "Be still, and know that I am God" (Psalm 46:10).

There is no need to even think of trying to change things that happened in the past. Too many of us still wallow in considering what we should have done rather than knowing that we are forgiven for our past foibles. In Christ, we are ready and able to move ahead in God's grace, mercy, and forgiveness. Lamentations 3:23 reminds us that His mercies "are new every morning." Wow, what a gift! As God's changed people, you and I can start right now, this minute, to look toward our unending life in the Lord!

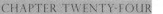

CHAPTER TWENTY-FOUR

ENCOURAGE, ENCOURAGE, ENCOURAGE!

The older I become, the more convinced I am that the three most significant priorities we older adults can have is to encourage, encourage, encourage!

Did you ever notice the word "age" right smack dab in the word "encourage"? Coincidence ? I don't think so!

I have a button that reads, "I was caught doing something right!" I like that button, although I must confess that no one gave it to me; I had to buy the silly thing. But the point is well taken. How many times do I bask in the ability to catch people doing things wrong? How many times do I play that great game, "gotcha"?

It is amazing to me how many times the word encourage is found in Scripture. The Lord and His disciples are so often found cheering people on, encouraging them to be who they are, in Jesus Christ. "Encouraging one another" (Hebrews 10:25); "to strengthen and encourage your faith" (1 Thessalonians 3:2 NIV); "encourage one another daily" (Hebrews 3:13 NIV); "By all this I am encouraged greatly" (2 Corinthians 7:4 NIV); "If it is encouraging, let him encourage" (Romans 12:8 NIV); and on and on.

Let us take a close look at what the word encourage can mean to us:

E–Enable. To encourage one another is to enable one another to think and dream and see a vision of what can be. It is easier to disable someone, but it is more rewarding, and fun, to enable them. Encouraging words enable people to recognize and use the gifts that God has given to them. Encouraging actions assist others to risk going out of their comfort zones to serve the Lord and those around them.

N–New. Help people to look at things in new ways. In the Lord, everything is new each day. Name what is new in your life today. Ask others what is new in their lives, and certainly move beyond saying "Jersey," or "York," or "Hampshire"! People can become discouraged when they do not see the Lord's forgiveness working in and through them to give them another day of grace and mercy, in the name of the Lord.

C–Children. Children are God's gifts to people of all ages. Celebrate the children in your life, even when they are too loud, or too hard to talk to, or do not even seem to be interested in you. Children bring us hope for the future.

Children give us a laboratory to use our listening skills—as well as our forgiving skills. We are not talking here about spending hours and hours with little ones (although that is not bad either, if you have the patience). No, we are talking about how our actions—the smiles, the listening ear, taking the time to talk, offering to drive a teenager to school or a little one to the park or ball practice—are all powerful testimonies to children of how the Lord is working through us. Try it, you'll like it. And they will too.

O–Open. We agree that God certainly opens doors for us, but how often do we close them for fear of getting a whiff of things we think we are not ready for? Try initiating a conversation with someone at the grocery store this week. Be more open-minded about a different political view. A friend once had two buttons made that he would distribute. One read, "You may be right." and the other one read, "I may be wrong." Now that is what I call being open to possibilities!

U–Unity. In this, the **United** States of America, there seems to be just too much **dis**-unity. A great way to encourage one another is to agree to disagree. We are united in faith in the Lord, and we had nothing to do with that happening. Our Baptism connects us with one another. We can celebrate our unity in Christ in the midst of our differences. There are so many differences between generations and cultures and lifestyles. To encourage one another does not mean we dumb-down our Christian core values or beliefs. It does not mean we support lifestyles that are contrary to our faith. To encourage one another does mean, however, that we are able to see and to sense the Lord continuing to work His love and forgiveness through us to those different folks around us. And watch His grace and love coming from them to you as well!

R–Remember. Try to grab hold of your past and remember one or two people who encouraged you when you were young. Go ahead, we all have met such people. Why did these people come to mind? Was it some big thing they did for you? Was it a gift they gave to you? I suspect that it may also be because of how they treated you. I am thinking right now of Mrs. Belma Boyer, my second grade teacher. She encouraged me by letting me know that she liked me. I remember Mr. Gust because he was one of the adults who would ever talk to me at worship on Sunday morning. Thanks, Mrs. Boyer! Thanks, Mr. Gust!

A–Available. Ministry in the Lord is all about availability. We need to take the time to be available to people, and that means sometimes making ourselves available when we do not really want to be. Pastor Charlie Mueller, Sr., has always been available to me during these past many years as we spend time weekly in our favorite office, St. Arbucks. Many adults make themselves available to students who have special needs. Others spend time child-watching, tutoring, and taking kids to the park. One of the best ways to love the Lord is to be available to His friends. Being available is such a strong indicator of the Lord living in and through us daily.

G–Grace. And it is all about grace. The grace of God, which you and I do not understand, is the gift that keeps on giving. It is the gift that keeps coming to us, despite how we act, look, or feel. It is God's gift to us each day. We encourage others because of God's grace in us and through us to others. Amazing Grace, indeed! Can you just hear "how sweet the sound" it is when God's promise moves in and through people through words of comfort, hope, and encouragement?

E–Easter. Now that's an easy one! We are encouraged people of God because we know how it all turns out, and so we go about Easterizing, in the name of the encourager Himself, Jesus Christ. We do not lose heart, we do not worry about our own condition and situation in life. No way! We encourage one another in the faith because the Spirit enables us to move out of our old, selfish ways of looking at life through me, me, me eyes. Instead we are able in faith to see God in Christ working in and through us to others. And as we encourage one another, we too are encouraged by that same Spirit, as the Lord works His wonder and power through all of us.

Philemon 1:7 wraps it up nicely with these words: "For

I have derived much joy and comfort from your love, my brother, because the hearts of the saints have been refreshed through you." How true, how true!

CHAPTER TWENTY-FIVE

DOWN WITH GROAN-UPS!

"Lightheartedness is the natural accompaniment to being justified solely by faith; that is, 'saved from being deadly serious.'"

(Martin Luther)

A number of recent studies throughout the United States claim that people over fifty are grumpier, complain more, and laugh less often than young people. ("Baby Boomers, the Gloomiest Generation," by D'Vera Cohn; Pew Research Center, December 20, 2010.) While little babies laugh more than three hundred times per day, teenagers chuckle only six times on average per day, while adults over sixty came in with a mere two to three guffaws within twenty-four hours.

How does that compare with your sense of laughter among your family and friends? Sounds a little high for some adults you know, maybe?

A long time ago, a wise, mature pastor in Michigan shared a "study" that made an impression on me. He claimed that the average child laughed and chuckled 150 times a day, while the average adult laughed and chuckled

15 times a day. Whether it is factual or not, it still sounds high for some of the adults we know, right?

Whatever the studies show, and however many youth and adults laugh or do not laugh around you, it is quite apparent that we need a national crusade titled, "Down with Groan-Ups!" Let's face it, there are just too many grouches living around us. Do you know someone without a sense of humor? (No pointing, please!) Of course you do! I suggest that the problem is not that some people have no sense of humor but rather that some feel they don't have permission to laugh, celebrate life, and take themselves less seriously.

Do people become more grumpy and serious because they grow older? Do people get the idea that being older means to be more mature and more serious? Perhaps therefore, without knowing it, some older people become less interesting and maybe even boring? At an event I attended years ago, I heard keynote speaker Michael Pritchard say, "You don't stop laughing because you grow old; you grow old because you stop laughing!" Here, the word *old* is being used in a negative context. I can see why many people also see *old* as negative if they assume that one aspect of growing old is to become less playful and more serious.

Have you ever noticed in the Scriptures that Jesus seems to play with the children and teach the adults? It seems that nowadays, the Church and society focus on teaching children and letting adults play as they may. In 1 Corinthians 13:11, Paul has something to say to us in this regard also: "When I was a child, I spoke like a child. . . . When I became a man, I gave up childish ways." Compare this to Jesus saying, "Whoever does not receive the kingdom of God like a child shall not enter it" (Mark 10:15). He is talking about the difference between *childish* and *childlike*.

What if Jesus was serious? What if children really are samples of true faith? What if living and being with younger people is also an invitation to belong to them and learn from them? What if adults who welcome and care for kids are actually hosting the living Christ? Author Les John Christie puts it this way: "If we hope to build relationships with young people, perhaps we adults would do well to relearn the lost language of youth—the language of play" (Les John Christie, *Best-Ever Games for Youth Ministry* [Loveland, Colorado: Group Publishing, Inc., 2005], 17).

We need to help our congregation and society redefine what being an adult is all about. It is not about getting more serious, more stern, and more set in our ways. It is not about telling younger people what life is all about. Instead, the aging process allows us to learn and relearn; it helps us to fail and to be forgiven in Christ in the process. It means to be transparent. It means that we are free not to have to pretend that we know all the answers to life's questions, because we do not and never will know everything. We don't need to know everything. The aging process helps us to be more human to those around us, rather than less human. To be human means to laugh and to cry, to learn and to fail, and to live each day in the forgiveness we have in Jesus Christ.

Perhaps older adults should have only two goals: to play more and to pray more. Sounds simple, but why not give it a try? Perhaps in all of the growing up we've been doing through the years, we have lost sight of what life is really about. It is not about who wins, who has the most toys in the end, and who has succeeded in life. Rather, we all have been gifted by God in Christ Jesus to receive forgiveness for all the messes we have made out of our lives and to live eternally with our Lord forever. This really "is most certainly true," as Martin Luther says in the Small Catechism.

A blind person once asked St. Anthony, "Can there be anything worse than losing eyesight?" He replied, "Yes, losing your vision" (anonymous Christian fable).

The Lord gives us His Word and His workers to teach us how to live well, age well, and die well, in the name of Jesus. We often lose sight of that, and yet when we go back to the divine service, where we hear His Word of forgiveness and receive His Holy Meal, He reminds us what they mean—that He bought our forgiveness and salvation and gives them to us freely!

An Australian friend of mine likes to say, "Laughter is the expression of unquenchable hope in the Lord." Well said, my friend, well said!

"Down with Groan-Ups"? No, I don't think so. I'd now rather say, "Up with Grown-Ups!" as the Lord continues to love us, even when we are "groan ups," and to move us along as we play and pray in His mercy and grace.

CHAPTER TWENTY-SIX

Okay, What Is So Good about Aging?

"Look, it took me a long time to get this old,
so I'm going to enjoy these 'good new days'!"

(Martha, eighty-two years old and still aging)

Aging is good because it is a gift from God! Aging is good because the Lord made us and works in and through us! Aging is good because as we age we know that for some reason the Lord is not through with us—yet!

My grandma, Minnie Schultz, wanted to die a long time before the Lord took her to heaven. As she rocked slowly back and forth in her brown, dusty rocker, she would get "the wogs," which meant that she could not keep that rocker still. She had nothing to do but rock and rock some more and wait for the Lord to take her home. Grandma was a complainer also. She complained that the soup was too hot or too cold. The room was too warm or too cold. The grandkids were too loud or too quiet.

Grandma lived in our home, in a little room off the kitchen. If I had ever asked her what she liked about aging, I am quite sure she would not have had much, if anything, to say. She was old. She was lonely. She was grouchy. She could not figure out why the Lord had forgotten her.

One day she was especially on a tirade, tearing into me because of something I had done or not done. As she growled and grumbled, I remember her looking at me and saying, "Richie, why doesn't the Lord take me to heaven?" I confess that I was frustrated and distraught about my own grandma chewing me out, and I should not have said what came out of my mouth at that time. I remember looking at her and yelling, "As grouchy as you are, I bet the Lord doesn't want to be with you in heaven!" From that day on, I knew deep down in my heart that I would no longer be in her will.

So, what really is so good about aging? Grandma Schultz, unfortunately, would not have much to add to this discussion. No doubt there are other Grandma Schultzes around as well: lonely, pensive, and rocking away each day with a case of "the wogs." The good news in all of this is that the Lord loves all of us grouches, including Grandma Schultz.

Here are some good things about aging:

1. Forgiveness is ours in the Lord at every age.

2. We have learned to realize, in faith, that life is not about me or you; it is about Him. For this, we are glad!

3. We have learned that hope in Christ always trumps our human experiences every time.

4. It is fun and affirming to learn that the priorities in life are faith in the Lord, family, friends, and forgiveness. (Plus a few other items we can all add!)

5. It is such a joy to be able to affirm and encourage other people of every age around us.

6. No worries about the fashion police! We can wear what we want and when we want to, even if it does not match or does not fit. (Where did I hang my Nehru jacket, anyway?)

7. We know who we are and, for the most part, we like who we are. We do not need to prove anything. We are who we are and what we are. We have gifts and limitations.

8. Our stress levels are lower, at least for the most part. We are more content, because our Savior lives!

9. We have discretionary time to volunteer, do nothing, visit people, watch sports, mentor the young, ask for help, and be ourselves.

10. We have become more stable and content. Our "what if" questions have been answered or, perhaps, forgotten.

11. We can spend more time thinking about other people than about ourselves.

12. We are better problem-solvers now, and we can more readily deal with issues and arguments. Experienced brains can more quickly make the right decisions.

13. We have confidence in what we are talking about, even if and when others do not agree.

14. We have many stories to tell that need to be told to people younger than us.

15. We have "been there, done that," which means that we are free to do things again and help others do things better than we ever could and feel good about it.

16. We know that people around us need us, even when it does not appear that they do.

17. We know that we are both caregivers and care receivers, depending on our own health and the health of those around us. We know that the Lord loves, forgives, and strengthens both the caregiver and the care receiver.

18. We realize now that we do not suddenly "get old" but that we are continually aging, and our attitude toward living makes all the difference in the world on this side of the resurrection.

19. We can pray every evening as we head for bed, "I can't wait to wake up in the morning!" If we do

not wake up the next morning, we know that this is okay also. (As someone once quipped, "Someday we're all going to wake up dead.")

20. We learn every day that the "aha's" of growing older always triumph over the "uh-ohs" of aging, because after every Good Friday, there is always an Easter!

To say it another way, we have grown to be able to see how big the cross of Jesus really is. We have experienced pain and disappointment and hurts galore. We know how it feels to be let down, shot down, and pulled down. We have lived through death and illness and dysfunctional families. We have endured hardships and false expectations and shattered dreams. Still the cross of Jesus is before us. Still we are able to "Lift High the Cross," because of His death and resurrection.

In 2 Corinthians 1:5–7, Paul says it this way: "For as we share abundantly in Christ's sufferings, so through Christ we share abundantly in comfort too. If we are afflicted, it is for your comfort and salvation; and if we are comforted, it is for your comfort, which you experience when you patiently endure the same sufferings that we suffer. Our hope for you is unshaken, for we know that as you share in our sufferings, you will also share in our comfort."

A grandpa was walking down the street with his little

grandson. As they passed a church, the grandpa looked up and pointed to the cross on the top of the church building. "Look, Aaron," he said. "Look at that big cross." The little guy looked up, saw the cross, and said, "That's not a big cross, Gramps, that's a small cross." "No," his grandpa repeated, "that's a big cross." "No way!" exclaimed the five-year-old, as they continued down the street.

That is the story, in a nutshell, of what's good about aging. The gift of aging allows us to see how big the cross really is in our lives. As all of the other hopes and dreams we have disappear through the years, through all of the disappointments and broken promises that we have experienced, through all of the little gods we've toyed with in our years of living, the aging process allows us to see how the cross of Jesus looms before us!

Perhaps that's what was missing in Grandma Schultz's life. Perhaps she never was able to work through the "uh-ohs" that made her grouchy. However, come to think of it, perhaps, through God's grace in Christ, she saw how big the cross of Christ really was, even in the midst of her grouchiness.

In our final conversation before she died, Grandma Schultz asked me, very seriously, why I thought that the Lord had not yet taken her to heaven. I remember responding, by the grace of God, saying something like, "Well, Grams, maybe He wants you around for a while just so you can talk to me and be my friend." I can still see her looking at me and almost smiling!

By the way, she did keep me in her will.

CHAPTER TWENTY-SEVEN

LEAVING A LEGACY:
FOR OTHERS OR IN OTHERS?

"If things get better with age, then I'm
approaching magnificent!"

(Author unknown)

As people age, they think and talk more about leaving a
legacy. A legacy, as you no doubt know, is defined as something enduring that is handed down to someone or established by someone, according to Mr. Webster. (Rumor has
it that Mr. and Mrs. Webster had a hard time communicating because it was very difficult for Mrs. Webster to get a
word in edgewise, but that is a legacy that we do not want
to pursue!)

Legacy language is certainly most appropriate and necessary. Many congregations, financial institutions, universities, and other agencies encourage older adults to consider leaving them a legacy. Many such entities have been
blessed immensely by these heartfelt gifts and striking support. I say amen and hooray to these efforts!

As we age—magnificently, by the way—it is helpful to
consider both leaving something *for* others as well as leav-

ing something *in* others. The good news is that we do not need to choose one or the other, but by God's grace, we can accomplish both. This is the beauty of seeing life through the eyes of John 10:10, abundantly and affirmingly. Seeing all of creation and all of our gifts as coming from God enables us to proclaim that abundance is really an attitude toward life in the Lord.

Although it is good for older adults to focus on leaving a legacy, it is important to clarify just whose legacy it is. We can and should be proud and bold about passing on a legacy, but in the process, we also need to be proud and bold to state strongly that what we are actually doing is serving our family and others. We serve them by purposely giving back to the Lord what the Lord has given us through our family and friends.

Now we must focus on the question, "What are you and I leaving *in* others?" while still thinking about the question, "What are you and I leaving *for* others?" Granted, it is perhaps difficult to separate them, but give it a try anyway. I would go even further and say that perhaps what we decide to leave for others helps to clarify and demonstrate what we actually are leaving in others. A case in point: Some friends of ours have a brilliant tradition. Each Christmas, they select a gift for each of their grandchildren out of their basement collection of "things good enough to keep but not good enough to use." They wrap each item and then have each grandchild select one, not knowing what lies inside the bright wrappings. The grandchildren are allowed to trade with each other before any of these "priceless" goodies are unwrapped. What a great Christmas tradition! Here, the grandparents are giving something to their grandchildren, but more important, they are leaving something *in* the grandchildren: that is, a sense of playfulness and humor that will last longer than the actual gifts. They are also cleaning out their basement in a highly creative way.

Another grandma and grandpa host a "Cousins Camp" each summer. Their grandkids are invited to spend a weekend with gram and gramps without their parents. They play, eat, laugh, tell stories, eat ice cream for breakfast, skip brushing their teeth, and stay up into the wee hours. What fun! What relationship-building! What an experience to leave as a legacy in those children! I imagine the parents do not mind their own weekend of one-on-one time either.

The Scriptures are filled with great examples of how ministry happens "from generation to generation" (Psalm 79:13). Inheritances were shared, stolen, misused, and lost, just like they are in these days. Beginning with Adam, we see how he shared with his son Seth and grandson Enosh (Genesis 4:26). We read about the conflict between Jacob and Esau (Genesis 25:27–34). Timothy knew all about the Lord, because his grandmother and mother shared their faith with him (2 Timothy 1:5). The stories go on and on and on.

So what are you and I going to leave in others, by the grace of God? We will joyfully leave in our family and friends a zest for life, a joy in knowing whose we are, and a delight in knowing that Christ Jesus has died and risen for each one of us. We will leave in others the knowledge that Christ has does this in and for them as well. We are called to leave in people the knowledge that we are all forgiven by Christ to leave a legacy for others and in others because of His living in us.

I like the button that states, "Jesus loves you!" Under these words, in small letters, it reads, "Of course, He loves everyone!" This is not a put-down at all. God indeed truly does love each one of us. Leaving a legacy for others and in others is all about sharing our faith in the one Lord, Jesus Christ.

A little girl was taught the song "Jesus Loves Me" by her grandmother. However, she never could get the words quite right. Instead of singing "Jesus loves me! This I know" (*LSB* 588:1), she instead would offer, "Jesus loves me! This I sow"! This little girl understood what it means to leave a legacy in others, in the name of Jesus.

CHAPTER TWENTY-EIGHT

GRANDPARENTING IS GRAND

> "God created grandparents because He knew
> He couldn't be everywhere at the same time!"
>
> (Author unknown)

Bad theology, but an interesting point! The Lord is indeed with us (Immanuel!) at all times. Perhaps the person who penned the quote above failed to realize that the Lord created each one of us to be "Jesus with skin on" to all those around us, young and old. Grandparents fill this role in exciting ways as they share their faith with grandkids in special ways.

Just ask grandchildren about grandparents and you might hear giggles and laughter as they say things such as these:

- "Grandparents are a lady and a man who have no children of their own; they like other people's."

- "Grandparents don't say 'hurry up!' "

- "Usually grandmothers are fat, but not too fat to tie your shoes."

- "Grandparents don't have to do anything except be there when we come to see them."

Grandparents are God's gift to children and to the world. They mentor, model, and minister to people of all ages and in all stages of life.

Today, thank the Lord for grandparents, whether you are one, or have one, or neither. If you are not a grandparent, become a "Rent-a-Grandparent" to some child in your life. If you are a grandparent, tell your grandkids how much you love them, every day, in every way—through notes, e-mails, phone calls, visits, hugs, and by just being there. Pray with them and for them also.

I'm reminded of a cute story about a little boy who was so excited when he came home from Sunday School one day. He bubbled, "Wow, do I have a great Sunday School teacher!" What's her name?" his father asked. "Well, I don't remember her name, but all I know for sure is that she is Jesus' grandma." "And how do you know that?" Dad inquired. "For two reasons," Billy said, still so excited. "First of all, because she has pictures of Him all over the room, and second, because she can't stop talking about Him." Oh, for the faith and joy of a child!

For those of us who are blessed to have grandparents in this world, take the time to thank the Lord, to reach out to them, and to let them tell their stories to you as you tell your stories to them. If you are a parent, encourage your grandkids to take the time to visit and listen and care for those gifts from God called Grandma and Grandpa.

Unfortunately, not all grandparents and grandchildren relate well. Many are disconnected because of broken homes, long distances, and all the other dysfunctions that happen because of sin. Author Maya Angelou states, "Today, people are so disconnected that they feel they are blades of grass, but when they know who their grandparents and great-grandparents were, they become trees, they have roots, they can no longer be mowed down."

Currently, over seven million children in the United States live with their grandparents. This is more than double the numbers of the 1970s. While this is an indication of the economy, broken homes, and other factors, older adults do need to be sensitive to these facts in order to be of help and support to children, parents, and grandparents in the process. I recall an experience a few years ago, when I was speaking on the joys and blessings on being a grandfather. What fun, how thrilling it was to be able to play and laugh with my grandkids, I shared. Immediately after I finished, I was greeted by a tearful woman who was bold enough to give me some feedback. She related that although she was glad that I and many other grandparents are enjoying our grandkids, she also wanted me to know that in her situation, she has never been able to see her grandchild, talk to him, or laugh with him, because her own daughter does not allow her to do so. What a tragedy, what heartbreak, and what a learning moment for me as well!

So, how are you doing with grandparenting, if indeed, you are grandparents? I trust you continue to love your grandkids, pray for them, and spend time with them, and that you are enabled by the Spirit to share your faith with them. The gift of being a grandparent, while filled with joy and excitement in so many ways, is truly an awesome experience and not to be taken lightly.

A few years ago, some of our grandkids agreed to write a book with me about grandparenting, of all things. Although it has not yet been completed, we have had a fun time dreaming with them about what they would say about their grandparents. To begin with, they quickly named the book *How to Raise Your Grandparents*. Not a bad start at all!

Here are a few glances at some of their thoughts and suggestions to grandparents:

1. Give us advice when we ask for it.

2. Keep in touch in as many ways as possible

3. Don't only tell us things, listen to us too.

4. Be available for us, but give us some space too.

5. Help us understand our parents.

6. Love us even when we mess things up.

7. Tell us stories, but don't make them too long.

8. Try to remember that we're just kids.

9. Be happy and playful around us.

10. Take us places, even if it's expensive.

Perhaps we as grandparents should make a list of how we see our role to our grandkids as well as to their parents—who just happen to be our kids and their spouses. My list would look like this:

1. Remember that I am not their parent, only their grandparent.

2. Be intentional about spending one-on-one time with each grandchild.

3. Treat each one differently according to his or her needs, while continuing to love each one equally.

4. The best way to support our grandchildren is to support, love, and forgive their parents.

5. Think out loud with them. Let them know how you feel about life, fears, family, and faith.

6. Laugh as often as possible with them.

7. Hug, high-five, or at least smile at and with them every time you see them.

8. Keep things confidential between you and each grandchild. What is discussed with a grandchild stays between you and the grandchild.

9. Go out of your way to do things with them and for them, and rejoice in this servant role.

10. Rejoice when you see some of the behaviors of your own children when they were young appearing in full color in the lives of your grandchildren: dirty shoes, messy rooms, long nights, and spilled milk!

11. Be a translator between your grandchildren and their parents. They live in a different culture together.

12. If you are separated by miles, work hard at keeping connected through phone calls, e-mails, Skype, texting, sending gifts, writing notes, visiting them for special and ordinary events, and by praying daily for them.

13. Be bold in telling the story of Jesus and His love for them and for you. Be intentional. Talk about the Lord in daily conversations. Share and talk about your blessings. Do as 1 Peter 3:15 encourages: "Always [be] prepared to make a defense to anyone who asks you for a reason for the hope that is in you."

14. Give and receive forgiveness to and from them. Keep them accountable for their actions, but always overpower them with God's unconditional love for them.

15. Did I mention—encourage them always in the joy and trust in the Lord!

One bonus suggestion: Always have a surprise for them in what you say and how you say it, in what you do and how you do it, in what you give and how you give it, and in who you are in the Lord. Lastly, "Whatever you do, in word or deed, do everything in the name of the Lord Jesus, giving thanks to God the Father through Him" (Colossians 3:17).

Hooray for grandparents and grandchildren! Let us work together by bringing all of God's people together to tell the story of Jesus and His love.

How do you spell *grandparent*? How about this:

G—Gift from God;

R—Remember them;

A—Affirm them;

N—Knowledge: Listen to their wisdom;

D—Do things together;

P—Party with them;

A—Ask them to help you;

R—Read to them and with them;

E—Eat meals together;

N—Never take them for granted; and

T—Tell them you love them, always!

Yes, grandparenting is grand. Take a grandchild or grandchildren to lunch today, and celebrate life in the Lord with them!

CHAPTER TWENTY-NINE

LIVING IN A DIFFERENT COUNTY TOGETHER AND SPEAKING A DIFFERENT LANGUAGE

Grandchild: "My grandma lives in a gated community, but they let her out once in a while."

Here is a list of words and phrases and how their meanings have changed over the past decades. Have fun with them, and think of some of your own examples.

DEFINITIONS: From Hippy to "Huh?"		
Word/Phrase	Then	Now
totally	for sure	I think it's a cereal.
pad	a place where someone lives	I would love to have an iPad.
hip	cool	Old people get them replaced.
threads	clothes	message boards
muckety-muck	an important person	I stepped in some yesterday.
whippersnapper	young person	I use one to trim the grass.
whoopsie-daisy	a surprise	My mom has those in her garden.

Word/Phrase	Then	Now
swell	wonderful	happens when I twist my ankle
mealtime	together around the table	fast food
skinny	inside information	not fat
Smokey	a cop	a bear that prevents fires
far out	unconventional but cool	How far?
boogie	to dance	I get them when I have a cold.
Shenanigans	questionable practices	an Irish pub
daddy-o	a cool older man	I think he's a rapper.
groovy	very pleasing	has a lot of grooves
heavy	something important, serious	someone needing a workout
decent	great or really great	going down
dynamite	awesome	used to blow up stuff
snappy	smart and fashionable	Was that one of the seven dwarfs?

Yes, language has certainly changed through the years. People of different ages use different languages. This is not to say that one generation is better than the other, just that they are different. Because of this, the very words we use to express ourselves often become barriers that prevent us from being understood.

We have a lot of fun as a family as the grandkids chuckle at some of our slang phrases and words. Oh, phooey! Oh, crumb! Doggone it! Rats! Okeydokey! Neat! Fiddlesticks! The list goes on and on. I'm not even mentioning some of the phrases our kids and grandkids use that make no sense to us either.

How should a grandchild know what a gated community is, anyway? How should I know that a grandkid wanted an iPod instead of a "me-Pod" when at one time I thought that a Kindle was something used to start a fire. (Now I understand that I can buy a Kindle Fire. No wonder I'm confused!)

As we delve deeper into the question of how generations communicate with one another, it becomes less of a joke and more of a serious and significant issue. All joking aside (or at least some joking aside!), the more we fail to communicate appropriately, the more difficult it is to bring generations together for family time, for telling stories, for worship, for study, and for fun. Look around you. Listen to those around you. All too often, older adults and younger people are living in a different country together and speaking a different language. For example, I recently heard an older woman remark that calling people who are unable to leave their homes *shut-ins* is not helpful. "How would you feel being called a shut-in?" she asked. Great point. She felt that the term *homebound* is more appropriate and positive. In similar fashion, what do older adults call some young people these days—*junior, kids, brats, juveniles*? The point is that all ages can improve on their perceptions of as well as their labeling of people of different ages.

Obviously, there have always been language barrier issues. Perhaps it is sometimes easier to communicate with people who speak a different language because we teach classes and we are intentional about listening more accurately to others of a different tongue. My friend Charlie knows a man who speaks nine different languages, and he speaks English the "goodest" of them all! In this fast-paced world, we often do not even use real words and phrases from any language because we are so busy abbreviating and adapting them so we can get on with texting or tweeting or Facebooking or linking or Googling or friending!

Perhaps a visit back to that first Pentecost can be helpful to this discussion. Isn't it amazing, as Acts 2 accounts for us, that people from all nations understood in their own language what was said? Acts 2:7–8 says it this way: "They were amazed and astonished, saying, 'Are not all these who are speaking Galileans? And how is it that we hear, each of us in his own native language?' " And what was it that they all heard? Verse 11 tells us, "We hear them telling in our own tongues the mighty works of God."

I don't wish to make light of the challenges and problems older adults as well as younger people have in understanding, listening, and communicating with one another. However, I suggest that perhaps a major role for older adults in this whole sphere of communicating is this: to make sure that what we say, how we say it, what we do, and how we do it all center on living out our faith in Jesus Christ. In other words, how can we help the Pentecost message become real in word and deed to those around us?

Of course it is necessary to understand one another's language. Of course we need to listen more intently and respond more hopefully. Of course we need to reach out to younger people by trying hard to grasp the new language and new technology of the day. However, let us never forget that the main reason we are attempting to communicate more appropriately with young people, as well as with older people, is to be able to share more effectively the message of Jesus Christ with those around us.

Another way to say this is that we need to acknowledge that we live in a cross-cultural world while strongly affirming our emphasis on Christ. It is Jesus' death on the cross that brings forgiveness and, therefore, joy to each one of us. It is by faith, which comes to us from the Holy Spirit, that we are enabled us to keep on communicating, as best we can, the message that people of all ages are redeemed, loved, and forgiven because of what Jesus did for us on His cross.

It is Jesus' death on the cross that forgives us every time we fail to communicate to others, to listen to others, or even to care about listening to others. It is the Holy Spirit's gift of faith in Christ that has freed us to go into the world with a message that crosses all nations and languages. It is the work of the Holy Spirit in us that empowers us to keep focused on Christ, who communicates to us even when we fail to communicate to Him.

Yes, we do have a lot of work to do as we struggle with words, changing definitions of words, and lack of knowledge in all this new technology. However, we live on this side of the resurrection, which assures us that God in Christ communicates with us and through us, through Word and Sacrament, that we are His! We are marked with the sign of the cross by water and Word; we are strengthened by the body and blood of Christ through bread and wine. He has claimed us as His own, and He communicates to us that we are His.

If that isn't enough, He daily assures us through faith that He is the Word. As we feebly try to communicate with finite words and phrases, the Lord Himself comes to us as the Word in our lives. Talk about communicating the message! He *is* the message.

One last story: A pastor was leading a children's message during an Advent service. He asked the question to the children: "Now, who can finish this Scripture passage: 'And the Word became . . .'?"

The kids just sat there, silent.

He asked again, "Come on now, who can finish this sentence: 'And the Word became . . .'?"

Nothing again. Silence is not golden in these kinds of situations!

The pastor felt the urge to move on, and so he said one last time, "Please, now, who will finish this sentence: 'And the Word became . . .'?"

Just then, over on the side, a little blonde girl bounced up and boldly shouted, "And the Word became . . . fresh!"

She was right! The Word, Jesus Christ, became flesh for us so we now can freshly tell His story of love and forgiveness. Christ became flesh, and now we share Jesus in fresh ways, as we become "Jesus with skin on" to those around us.

The Word, Jesus Christ, communicates in and through us. For this, we are glad!

CHAPTER THIRTY

THE GENERATION GAP REVISITED

Some of us are old enough to remember the so-called generation gap television dramas of the 1960s as the youthful "hippies" conflicted with the establishment of the day. Through clothes, music, words, and lifestyles, the two generations always seemed to be clashing in homes, on the streets, campuses, and even in congregations. I think I still have my "Make Love Not War" T-shirt.

A few years later, I partnered with other educators to develop a model to help bring these two generations together to talk, share, listen, and, we hoped, find common ground. The name of this model was creative, I thought; who would not be interested in learning how to communicate more effectively with the other generation? It was called "Bridging the Gap" and emphasized how God's people actually are bridge-builders between young and old, because of what God in Christ Jesus has done for all of us. But it was not an easy sell. Young people had more important things to do than sit around and to get to know some of the over 30 adults; and the 30s and older crowd did not see much point in listening to these kids either, since what was really needed, they insisted, was for someone to tell them to shape up and change their lives and lifestyles.

I thought then, and I still contend, that there never really was a generation gap, but rather what we experience is an "attitude gap" between people of all ages.

One of our granddaughters, Rachel (who is our favorite granddaughter named Rachel!), is helping me to be more sensitive and aware of how us older folks might communicate and care more for and with younger folks. The first way that she is being helpful to me is that she still allows me to join her at a favorite St. Arbucks. Perhaps without my knowing it, she might case the joint before we enter to see if any of her friends are lurking there; nevertheless, she allows me to sit at the same table and talk with her. These are special times for me and have reinforced that a significant way to bridge the gap between generations is to simply put them within ministry range of each other. Rachel and I certainly have differences of opinion, but as we continue to take time to care and listen to each other, we both will mature and grow in our faith and life. We'll get to know each other better too.

It would be revealing to take a survey to find out how many adults regularly sit and talk with people thirty or forty years younger and how many young people take the opportunity to go one-on-one with a 70-year-old on a regular basis. The point of all this is not to confirm how differently 20-year-olds and 70-year-olds think and feel, but to be intentional about listening and sharing ideas, feelings, joys, frustrations, doubts, hopes with someone who is willing to listen and care, even if we do not agree with everything being said.

But there is much more involved in the quest to bridge the gap between people.

A recent blog post said it well: "We tweet, we text, we e-mail. Everybody's chatting, but is anybody listening?" ("Where Conversation Goes from Here," by David Dudley, http://newsletter91507.blogspot.com/2010/02/where-conversation-goes-from-here.html. Accessed March 23, 2012.) These, indeed, are challenging times especially in terms of how we communicate and teach others to communicate by how we communicate. Daniel Menaker, who crusades for traditional, face-to-face connections between people, states, "Not to be apocalyptic, but I'm very worried. There's a special obligation to be available in a public space." He adds that this is not just a public irritation, it's a cultural crisis. ("Where Conversation Goes from Here," by David Dudley, http://newsletter91507.blogspot.com/2010/02/where-conversation-goes-from-here.html. Accessed March 23, 2012.) Dr. Richard Schwartz, Harvard MD, puts it this way: "We move a lot, and that widens and weakens our connections with others. Technology creates this same widening and weakening." ("Where Conversation Goes from Here," by David Dudley, http://newsletter

91507.blogspot.com/2010/02/where-conversation-goes-from-here.html. Accessed March 23, 2012.)

So where do we go from here? How do we handle the iPods, texting, e-mail blasts, Facebooks, Plaxo, Tweets, LinkedIns, and on and on? Shall we prohibit them? Endorse them? Forget about them?

Or, shall we continue to patiently bridge the gap between generations? Shall we confess to one another that we do not have the answers, that we're not sure where all this is leading? Shall we commit ourselves, at the very least, to attempt to build "We-Pods" to counter and build on all of the "I-Pods" around us?

Rachel and I will probably never agree on how important texting really is. She will no doubt continue to be humored at how long her grandpa takes to text a four word message to her. Our St. Arbucks talks will continue to be interrupted by her cell phone "music de jour." Despite it all, my hope and prayer is that we learn from each other, listen to each other, care for each other, and love and forgive each other, as we keep in ministry range of each other.

And as we connect with people, one-on-one, in our homes, schools, classrooms, churches, and communities, may we communicate in every way possible that we have a Lord who continues to communicate His love and forgiveness to each one of us through His Word and Sacrament. And even when technology and distance and priorities and multi-tasking and self-centeredness get in the way, may God's Spirit continue to bring hope and forgiveness and peace and joy and the ability to start over again to communicate what life in the Lord is all about.

Author Leonard Sweet says that in today's world, T.G.I.F. now means "Texting, Google, iPad, and Facebook." Maybe so, but I strongly urge all of us, young and old, to urge each other to affirm that T.G.I.F. means "Thank God I'm Forgiven!"

Just last night I saw in one of the St. Arbucks I frequent, a sign that reads something like this, "To clasp the hands in prayer is the beginning of an uprising against the disorder of the world."

Sounds like a great plan to bridge the gap . . . in the name of Jesus!

(Reprinted with permission from *LE Journal*, August, 2010)

CHAPTER THIRTY-ONE

WHO SAYS OLDER ADULTS ARE TECHNOLOGICALLY CHALLENGED?

Gramps: "The TV remote isn't working."

Grams: "That's because you're trying to use your cell phone to change channels."

Gramps: "Oh, so that's probably why my cell phone wasn't working either!"

It is possible to teach older adults new tricks, and older adults are indeed savvy when it comes to high-tech sorts of things. As proof positive that we older adults are "cool"—which means "with it," I think!—here is a fun list of some of the possible e-mail addresses of older adults:

- Grandmaandgrandpaalways@odds.net

- Windycitygrandma@hair.net

- Emptynesters@last.com

- Grandpacantsleep@night.com

- Weliketostay@home.com

- Grandmacanbeatu@cards.com

- Wearsomeshorts@least.com

- Welovetowin@bingo.net

- Hardtopay@tension.net

- Grandmaisgood@baking.com

- Weenjoypotlucks@church.com

- Spoiledgrandkids@Christmastime.com

- Grandmaisshopping@themallagain.net

- Imgolfing@thecountryclub.com

- Grandpaisworking@hisdesk.com

(By Bob Bimler. Used by permission.)

If this is not enough proof, further "research" has discovered these top Web sites being used and operated by none other than older adults. Internet police, here we come:

- www.ivefallenandicantgetup.com

- www.wherearemykeys.com

- www.bingo.com

- www.whatdidyousay.com

- www.grayhairrocks.com

- www.slowdriverslivelonger.com

- www.grandkidsarecool.com

- www.whyareyouhere.com

- www.idontneedyourhelp.com

- www.ihavepantsolderthanyou.com

- www.iliveinfloridanow.com

- www.itwonthurttocallmesometime.com

- www.pleaseturnoffthelights.com

- www.nineoclockisbedtime.com

- www.whereismypolyesterleisuresuit.com

(By Bob Bimler. Used by permission.)

In all seriousness, all of the new technology that is changing every day can be a challenge for us older people. However, this challenge can be turned into an opportunity by asking younger people for help in this area of our lives. What a great chance to get to know teenagers better! What a great chance to listen to their stories and hear about their ups and downs! What a great chance to share our faith in the Lord with them as they share their faith with us!

I am always amazed as I read about the ministry of Jesus as He moved throughout Palestine, proclaiming and teaching and healing people of all ages. He was an expert at asking questions, sensing the needs of people, and listening to them. He did not have grandchildren to talk to and play with, but He did indeed play and laugh with the young as well as the old. As a matter of fact, I think He may have spent as much or more time playing with children and teaching adults than we do in our congregations.

Through technology, young people can help us be more aware of the present, the now of life. They have not yet experienced the types of things we have already gone through. Perhaps they have not yet envisioned what the Lord has in store for them. They live in the now, and they can help us relate to the now as we bring our past experiences into their lives.

Young people and technology can also keep us older adults humble. We do not have all the answers. In fact, we have many questions. Young people can help us sort out when an experienced answer is needed, when a question is helpful, and when we need to keep quiet and listen to their thoughts and particular expertise. As a matter of fact, for us to be humble is quite a gift to give to those younger than we are. It shows that people of all ages learn throughout their lifetime. It shows that we are real, genuine, and transparent, as well as sinful human mistake-makers. What a gift we give to young people when we show that even we older folks do not have it all together!

I am reminded of the story about the young man attempting to help his grandparents fix their computer. Grams and Gramps have worked on it for hours and have finally decided to ask their fifteen-year-old grandson for help. He comes over to their home, takes a look at the situation, and coyly says, "Well, the first thing we ought to do is plug it in!" Some helpful and hopeful relationships were formed that day.

Asking others for help and support is healthy and a

powerful way to affirm the other person. It means that we believe that we ourselves are worthy of receiving help and that the person being asked is a valuable part of our lives. In addition, asking is an act of love. It affirms God's design of providing help and support through the presence of others in our lives.

Technology does not need to drive people away from one another and make our lives more impersonal. Technology can be used as an instrument to connect and reconnect with people of all ages. For example, Facebook has become a social network for both young and old. Sure, misuse and inappropriate communications go on, but that happens with every form of technology and it does not detract from the value that this and other new media provide. I like Facebook because it helps me connect with my grandchildren as well as with some classmates from way back when. I also agree that Facebook provides me with far too much information, but to think about it, I never read the entire daily newspaper either.

So thank the Lord daily for technology, whether or not we understand it or even use it. Thank the Lord that there is yet another vehicle we can use to keep connected with people young and old. This is what the Church is all about. We are made for togetherness, for community, for family, for assisting one another, and for being available to others. We are the Church, together, to bring the Gospel to others through every network of interdependence, hope, and for-giveness, all in the name of Jesus.

Let us all pray that we have questions and problems with our electronic gizmos and gadgets so we can ask a younger person to assist us. I think I will unplug my computer right now!

CHAPTER THIRTY -TWO

That's What Friends Are For

" 'A friend in need is a pest'? No, a friend in need is the best!"

(Martha, eighty-one years old)

The older I grow, the more I remember about my younger days. For example, I remember listening to my mom sadly comment that all of her friends were dying. She was around seventy-five years old at the time. What I remember the most about our conversation is that I snapped back at her, "Well, just go out and make new friends!"

I was not old enough or smart enough then to understand that my mom was actually struggling with loneliness. My dad had died when he was fifty, so my mom had been on her own for many long years. My flippant response to her was unhelpful and way off base. It is very difficult, especially at that age, simply to go out and collect some new friends from the highways and byways.

Friendship is such a strong and wonderful gift that the Lord gives to each of us. "Friends don't let friends drink and drive," but friends do allow friends to drink in the beauty of trust and companionship through the years. As we grow older, the need and desire grows for someone to be there for us to talk to, listen to, cry and laugh with, and simply be there. Friendship is a substantial ingredient in growing older gracefully. Studies show that friendship is a key factor in older adults living healthy and significant lives. Ask those older adults around you about the importance of friends in their lives. My guess is that they will tell you that the gift of friendship ranks right near the top.

The beauty of friendship is exactly what the Church is all about. God has created us to live in relationships with others. The holy huddle, the Church, is comprised of people of all ages who need others around them to share with, care for, celebrate with, and learn and love together.

In fact, God created us to live in relationship with our best Friend—Jesus Christ. Romans 5:10 reminds us what true friendship is: "While we were enemies we were reconciled to God by the death of His Son. . . . More than that, we also rejoice in God through our Lord Jesus Christ, through whom we have now received reconciliation."

Matthew 18:20 reassures us that "where two or three are gathered in My name, there am I among them." The Church again becomes the center of our lives as we reach out to and through others in Christ's name. Even Ecclesiastes 4:9–10 gets into the discussion about friends: "Two are better than one, because they have a good reward for their toil. For if they fall, one will lift up his fellow. But woe to him who is alone when he falls and has not another to lift him up!"

The Ecclesiastes passage reminds me that some older people are quite sensitive about the word *fall*. "Always say 'Happy autumn,' a friend of mine says. "Never say 'Happy fall' to an older person."

That is what friends are for! To help us laugh, to help us not take ourselves so seriously, and to be there when we need to have someone close to us as a sign of Christ's presence in us. Friends lift us up when we fall, no matter what season it is!

Think of some of your friends, both from your earlier days as well as right now. Name them. Thank them. Thank God for them. How were they there to pick you up when you had fallen? Who was it that brought a smile to your face at a time you needed it most? Who was there to remind you of God's love in Christ as you struggled with fear and doubt and loneliness? Yes, friends do let friends drink in the blessings and gifts of the Lord.

Friendships are also so crucial in marriage. To have your spouse as your best friend is not only sweet but also a blessing. Friendships are indeed tested daily in marriage. Hazel and I have been married for more than fifty years— and that is in a row! What a ride! We can proudly announce that through all the myriad of years, we have never had an argument; however, we have had many, many, many constructive conflicts. Friendships help to weather the storms, overcome the tsunamis, and keep one another warm when the journey gets bogged down.

A friend of ours tells this story of a husband and wife of many years. The wife was sipping on a glass of wine while sitting on the patio with her husband, and she said, "I love you so much. I don't know how I could ever live without you." Her husband asked, "Is that you or the wine talking?" She replied, "It's me—talking to the wine!" Friendships allow us to laugh and cry as we live and love together in the Lord.

Friendships come and friendships go. My mom was right. All her friends were dying. I did not understand that because I had not experienced the death and loss of many friends. Now I am beginning to understand better the gift of friendship and how essential it is for each of us to be a friend to others as well as to have friends. Our role as we grow older is to be intentional about taking the time to spend time with people and to develop other friendships for ourselves. Perhaps this even means that we force ourselves to spend time with people even when we do not feel like it. Perhaps it means that we insist, evangelically of course, that others around us who may be struggling with loneliness and the loss of friends come with us to church and community events. Perhaps it means we take Ecclesiastes seriously and reach out to people around us in order to pick them up when they fall.

I'm reminded of this story of a man who was waiting in line at a coffee shop for his morning cup of java. He seemed quite anxious and in a hurry, so the young woman in front of him offered to let him order before she did. The gentleman accepted the offer and mentioned that he was in a hurry to get to the nursing home to have breakfast with his wife. "Does she get angry when you are late?" the woman asked. The man responded, "No, not at all. You see, she has Alzheimer's, and she no longer recognizes me." The woman was surprised and asked him, "And you still go there every morning, even though she doesn't know who you are?" The man smiled and said, "She doesn't know who I am, but I still know who she is."

This is what friendship is all about. We love and care for our friends because our Friend, the Good Shepherd, loves and cares for us, and He always knows our name.

Yes, what a friend we have in Jesus, and what a Jesus we have in friends!

CHAPTER THIRTY-THREE

OLDER ADULTS:
THE MINISTERING ONES

"The best classroom in the world is at the feet
of an elderly person."

Older adults of all ages have exciting ministries in the Lord. Just take a look around you and see! Watch Ken, who has been mentoring that eight-year-old in school. Observe Judy and the other dedicated women who serve meals at the shelter each week. Wave to Andy, who visits your neighbor down the street and brings her a snack (and even a beer). Thank Barb for volunteering at the nature site regularly. Listen to Leo as he shares his excitement at bringing turtles into the classroom for little kids to touch and enjoy. And then there is Larry, who is so faithful as a weekly usher in your congregation. No one can forget Lucille, who brings her happy laugh and smiling face to the Lutheran Home each week as a volunteer. "I'm here to bring cheer!" she boasts, and she does.

There are so many other unsung heroes in the older adult world. They serve people because they like people. They serve people because they know the Lord loves them.

They serve people because, as Margaret states, "I get so much more out of helping others than they get from me. I do it because I need to do it!" They serve people because people need to be served.

So many of the volunteers in our church body and society are older adults. Why? First, because the number of older adults continues to grow. Older adults also have more discretionary time than people younger than them. Of course, younger adults have always been involved, but many of them also have work and school commitments. Another exciting model of serving others is when people of all ages team up to serve together, such as on a mission team or a church advisory group or by coaching a sport.

Another major reason that a greater number of older adults are using their time to serve and be with others is because they have found out that they have many gifts to share with others. Others do it for the joy and affirmation they themselves receive. George, a hospital information guide, confesses, "Just one person saying to me, 'You've made my day,' makes my day!"

As an aside, but a very important one, a comment needs to be made on an emerging trend that is becoming more evident in some congregations. It is the mindset that we go to church not to serve but to be served. We want to be served our kind of music, our kind of children's message, our kind of youth ministry, and even our kind of older adult ministry. If we are not being served what we want, we then go grazing in other churches to find what we want. Now is the time for people, including older adults, to bring to their churches a resurgence of the biblical model of serving and discipleship. I remember a meeting in a congregation recently, during which an older woman was sharing her frustrations about the lack of events and focus on older adult ministries. As she rambled on, she said, "We need someone in this church to do something for older adults!" All of a sudden, like a bolt from the sky, she stopped speaking, put her hands on her face, and exclaimed, "Hey, I'm an older adult. Maybe I can start doing something in this church for us!" We love and serve others because Jesus loves and serves others through us. It is our time to serve and not merely be served.

People of all ages are finding out more and more that one of the best gifts they can offer to others is the gift of presence. Just being there to listen to someone, assist someone, or talk to someone makes such a difference in people's lives. Perhaps our society could use "fewer gifts and more presence" in certain families and relationships. It is helpful to Wilma, the widow down the street, when a group of teenagers come to her house to cut the grass and rake the leaves, but their time with her is perhaps even more important than the efforts they give in her yard. Their presence at her home is a gift that cannot be underestimated. As some might say, "The gift of their presence is priceless."

An emerging model in congregations, social ministry organizations, and communities these days provides opportunities for older adults, the sixty- to seventy-year-olds, to be of specific help and friendship to those adults around them who are even older, the seventy-five- to ninety-year-olds. As the trend continues for keeping elderly people in their own homes for as long as possible, the need for these younger older adults to be of support and assistance to them is quickly increasing.

Who do you have in your life that is available to talk with you, listen to you, be with you, encourage you, and welcome you as a friend and equal? This need for companionship and friendship is not age-limited. We are created for relationships. People of all ages need to be connected within ministry range of others. Who can you go to when you need counsel and guidance; who can be with you to affirm you and cheer you up? The presence of a person to be there for you is a powerful need as well as a powerful gift from the Lord. If you have such a person around you, rejoice and be glad. If you do not have this gift near you, start looking and asking for someone who can bring you the Lord's presence in this way. Ask a member of your congregation, ask a neighbor, or call someone to help make this happen. Yes, we need "fewer gifts and more presence" in our lives, starting with me and you.

Here is a story that caps off what life is all about. An

old, tired dog wandered into the yard of an eighty-year-old man. The dog looked well-fed and was evidently from a home that was taking good care of him. The dog came over to the man, and the man gave him a few pats on his head. The dog then followed the man into the house, slowly walked down the hall, curled up in a corner, and went to sleep.

An hour later, the dog woke up and went to the door, and the old man let him out. The very next day, the dog was back again. He walked inside the house, resumed his spot in the hall, and again slept for an hour. This continued off and on for several weeks. One day, the man decided to pin a note on the dog's collar that said, "I would like to find out who is the owner of this wonderful dog and ask if you are aware that almost every day your dog comes to my house for a nap."

The next day, the dog once again arrived for his nap with another note pinned to his collar. The note said, "He lives in a home with six children, two of which are under the age of three. He's trying to catch up on his sleep. Can I come with him tomorrow?"

Thank the Lord for people of all ages, and especially older adults, who are caregivers and gifts to others as they bring the presence of the Lord, in the flesh, to people young and old!

Here is a responsive reading that can be used individually or in a group to reflect and celebrate our ministries together:

Older Adults, the Ministering Ones

Happy are those who suffer with the very young, the very old, and the very lonely, *for they have compassion.*

Happy are those who greet the world with smiles, laughter, and anticipation, *for they have courage.*

Happy are those who live not for themselves but for others, *for they have freedom.*

Happy are those who listen and learn and extend their hands, *for they have understanding.*

Happy are those who speak gently and live humbly, *for they have dignity.*

Happy are those who give simply and love deeply, *for they have sincerity.*

Happy are those who live intensely and sing
through life the praises of the risen Christ,
for they have awareness.

Happy are those who have compassion and courage, freedom and dignity, understanding, sincerity, and awareness,
for they are unique.

Happy are those who at times forget their priorities, focus too much on themselves, react inappropriately to others, and sometimes even make a big mess of things, *for they are forgiven!*

CHAPTER THIRTY-FOUR

Go Ye Forth . . . and Connect!

Chad: "Grandma, you sure have flabby arms!"

Grandma: "Chad, that's not nice to say. If you can't say something nice, you shouldn't say anything at all."

Chad: "Sorry Grams. I meant to say your arms are nice and flabby!"

Older adults love to connect with their families, even when conversations like this spring up. The *2012 Statistical Abstract of the U.S.* provides ample evidence of this. For example, in 2010, among 78.8 million households, 16.9 million included family members who were 65 years of age and older. Another finding was that 56 percent of people 64 and older see their children at least weekly and 40 percent see their grandchildren that often as well. And here is a clincher: 90 percent of the respondents felt revitalized when they spent time with their families and 70 percent wanted to connect with their families more often through the year. (U.S. Census Bureau, *2012 Statistical Abstract of the U.S.,* http://www.census.gov. Accessed March 23, 2012).

Besides person-to-person, how do older adults connect with their family members? Mostly by landline phones (78 percent) followed by cell phones (54 percent) and e-mail (37 percent). My hunch is that more and more older adults are using Facebook to stay connected as well.

Ask an older adult, especially a grandparent, what one of their favorite things to do is and I think most will say, "Be with my kids and grandkids."

What do your congregation, community, and family do to bring families together? How can we serve as caring connectors with older adults within their own families? In this same U.S. Census Bureau survey, almost a third of the older adults saw their role in their families as being the "connector." Perhaps our congregation's role can be to more intentionally support and affirm older adults as they serve as the connectors within their own households.

Interesting also were the other roles older adults saw themselves having within their families. Besides the 32 percent who said connector, here are the other significant responses:

Peacemaker: 19 percent

Historian: 17 percent

Entertainer: 8 percent

These findings might spark an energizing discussion topic around a family meal, especially if there are older adult peacemakers at the table!

As our population continues to age, there will be more older adults around, both to connect with family members and to be cared for by family members, as well as other community and congregation caregivers. This fact is both a challenge and an opportunity for each of us. As a matter of fact, do you realize that right now there are more people in the world who are 65 and older than the total number of people who have lived to be 65 in the history of the world. An astounding fact, but true!

Families continue to be the connecting point for many people. Ozzie and Harriet no longer live next door, but family relationships, core values, and the joy of telling and re-telling stories still prevail. Granted, many families are fractured and fragmented. Many children and adults are still invisible to so many of us who are blessed with strong family traditions and values. What is needed is something that more and more older adults can provide, and that is exactly what the studies mentioned above indicate: older adults can be freed up to be connectors, peacemakers, historians, and even entertainers, not only in their own families but also in other families and community agencies that so desperately need these gifts.

It is one thing for you and me to thank the Lord for our families and continue to work hard at developing and growing relationships within them. However, it is quite another challenge for us to offer our time, our gifts, our own lives to be a connector for other people. As God's redeemed, we need to see all people, throughout the world, as our brothers and sisters. Christ has brought us together as His one family as we minister to each other in one large human network, while at the same time loving and learning and listening and laughing with those around us.

Grandparents and other older adults are the perfect connectors in today's society. We are present, available, tested, experienced, and we need to be needed, involved, and fulfilled by others. What a perfect combination! And what a challenging challenge! The Lord is opening up the mission field right before our very eyes, and we do not have to hop on a plane to serve. We respond to the challenge of connecting people not because we "gotta" do it, but because we "get" to, all in the name of the Lord. And we do it joyfully because, after all, it is the Lord Himself who continues to connect to us, through the Word and Sacraments, so we are able to help connect others to the cross and the empty tomb.

One last note: Thinking again about the various roles in which we are involved—connector, peacemaker, entertainer, historian—I must share this closing story:

> The coach called one of his nine-year-old baseball players aside and asked, "Do you understand what cooperation is? What a team is?" The little boy nodded in affirmation. "Do you

understand that what matters is whether we win or lose together as a team?" The little boy again nodded yes. So the coach continued, "I'm sure you know when an out is called, you shouldn't argue, curse, attack the umpire or call him names. Do you understand that?

The little boy nodded again. The coach continued, "And when I take you out of the game so another boy gets a chance to play, it's not good sportsmanship to call your coach a dummy, is it?" Again, the little boy nodded.

"Good", said the coach. "Now, would you go over there and explain all that to your grandmother?"

Even when we connect with others in less than promising or helpful ways, we live in the forgiveness that Christ Jesus continues to shower upon us, ready to connect, ready forgive, ready to celebrate and laugh together in the Lord.

CHAPTER THIRTY-FIVE

Taking the Risk

> "As Eugene Peterson once put it, 'We wake into a world we didn't make, and into a salvation we didn't earn.' Grace is underway before we even reach for the cornflakes."

(Peter W. Marty, "The World of Grace." *The Lutheran*, December 2010, http://www.thelutheran.org/article/article.cfm?article_id=9556 [accessed January 9, 2012].)

What are we waiting for? Go ahead: take the risk of living and loving in the Lord!

Older adults, just like all God's people in Christ, live in God's grace. It is ours, right now! Perhaps you are like me: I know this in my head, but I am so cautious about living out my life freely and fully for other people. Some mornings, I am even afraid to reach for the cornflakes, lest I spill them all over the kitchen floor.

A tightrope walker was doing his act across Niagara Falls. Not only was he making his way across the wire blindfolded, but he was also pushing a wheelbarrow. When he got to one side of his journey, he asked the crowd if someone would like to hop in the wheelbarrow for a free return trip across to the other side.

The people started cheering and hollering for him to

continue his trip, but no one volunteered to get into the wheel barrow. "You can do it! You can do it!" they shouted, but no one joined him in his adventure. No one doubted he could do it, but no one trusted him enough to get into the wheelbarrow.

It isn't that our older-adult years ask us to get into the wheelbarrow of life. It's that we are already in the wheelbarrow, but we do not know it. When we were younger, perhaps we were cautious about getting involved in the lives of other people. We had jobs to do, kids to raise, and bills to pay. After all, we must be responsible for what the Lord has given us to support and do. Perhaps we reasoned that first we should take care of ourselves and our family, and then, if we have time and energy, we could become more involved in the community, the congregation, and the world.

I readily relate to this with much guilt and strong feelings. In my earlier years, I was so intent on trying to be all things to all people. I was so locked into my ministry position that I felt guilty every time the phone rang at home while I was there; after all, I should be at my church office or making calls or visiting someone. A former church staff person and I would play the game of "who can get to the office first." If I arrived at 6:00 a.m., he would be there at 5:30 a.m. the next day. Okay, I'd show up at 5:00 a.m. the next day—and he would pull in at 4:30 a.m. the following day. No one wins this kind of game.

Talking about God's grace and cornflakes—why, I didn't even take the time to open the cereal box.

Our older adult years are a time for you and me to step back, review our lives and behaviors, and have a loud laugh. We must either laugh or feel guilty and broken the rest of our lives. I choose laughter! I laugh not because I am trying to forget all the misdirection and wrong priorities of my past but because I am forgiven and redeemed by what Christ has done for me and you. In a real sense, I have not chosen to get in the wheelbarrow of life—the Lord put me there. Now all I need to do is enjoy the ride over the abyss of life, realizing there still are bumps along the wire but committed in Christ to hang in there for this wild ride.

We older adults still have much on our minds: finances, health, family, future, purpose in life, and reaching out to the lonely, the lost, the last, and the least. We do not sit passively in the wheelbarrow. We serve people, care for people, and love those around us, knowing all the while that the Lord is still pushing and nudging us along. Every day of our trip, we know that He is in control, which really frees us up to serve others. Have you ever tried to play God? It's tough work, isn't it? It is a 24/7 commitment. But the beauty of God's grace is that we do not have to play God. We already have one: the Triune God.

Someone once said, or should have said, "We can pretend that we care, but we can't pretend that we're there." We are where we are, right now, in the hands of the Lord.

One last point: our older adult years are also wonderful years to step back and enjoy life, not because we have earned it but because the Lord has given us these years to live, enjoy, serve others, and worship Him. Perhaps sometimes it is impossible to believe that the Lord wants us to relax and enjoy His creation. He has given us today to be a day of wonder, delight, and celebration. It is so unbelievable, that it can become a burden to consider life as a play day with God and others. Go ahead: enjoy this day, and enjoy the ride. We are in the wheelbarrow, and we are in God's good hands as we continue on our journey of joy.

Don't forget to enjoy the cornflakes!

CHAPTER THIRTY-SIX

LOOK AT ALL THE FAMOUS OLDER PEOPLE!

"I don't feel a day over 84."
(George H. W. Bush, as quoted by the Associated Press, June 12, 2009)

The newspapers often feature people in their eighties and nineties still going strong and performing exciting and surprising feats. A woman from Indiana recently went skydiving on her eighty-first birthday. Everything went well except her landing. She ended up in the hospital with a broken ankle, but she still insisted that the experience was one of the highlights of her life. (Remember the old saying, "You do not need a parachute to go skydiving. You only need a parachute to go skydiving twice.")

Then there is former President George H. W. Bush, who since he turned seventy-five celebrates every fifth birthday by jumping out of a plane—with a parachute, of course. When asked why he does this, he remarked, "Just because you're an old guy, you don't have to sit around drooling in the corner. Get out and do something. Get out and enjoy life" (MSNBC.com, "Elder Bush Completes Parachute Jump," http://www.msnbc.msn.com/id/31301377/ns/

politics-more_politics/t/elder-bush-completes-birthday-parachute-jump/#.Twub7_JkjPY [accessed January 9, 2012]).

Well said, President Bush! His wife, Barbara, was asked how she felt about her husband enjoying this annual event. With her humor in high gear, she said, "George jumps out over a field where there is a church. That's a good thing, because it won't be too far to move him!" Touché, Mrs. Bush!

You have heard and seen these figures before: George Bernard Shaw was ninety-four when one of his plays was introduced. Ben Franklin framed our constitution when he was eighty-one. Grandma Moses was seventy-six when she began to paint, and her work was discovered when she was seventy-eight. Albert Schweitzer was seventy-seven when he received the Nobel Peace prize. The list goes on and on and on.

The Scriptures also portray many older people serving the Lord in a variety of exciting ways: Noah, Moses, and Abraham, not to mention Methuselah. We thank the Lord that He worked His miracles and wonders in ancient days as well as today. People of all ages have been blessed and taught and guided by the wise sages of old, the giants of our faith, and the leaders of our country and the world.

Where does that leave us? We honor and boast and recognize these well-known older adults who have done astonishing things, but what about us? I doubt that I will ever jump out of an airplane, at least voluntarily. I cannot even sing a song well, let along write one. No one will ever ask me to renew the United States constitution. Nevertheless, the Lord is calling you and me to serve Him in marvelous ways.

The only difference between these famous folks and us is that most of us will never end up with a Nobel Peace prize or a Hall of Fame medal or a Super Bowl ring—and that is okay. That's only a problem if we think that unless we become "super seniors" and do something that changes the world, then we have not reached our potential in life. That is far from the truth. That objective is not what life is all about.

I still remember when our kids entered the family cat in a "Best Cat" contest in St. Louis, years ago. I remember how proud they were when they came home with Spring and proudly announced that she had won second place. Wow, what an honor! They then mentioned, softly, that the other cat won first place.

You and I know that life is not about winning and being the best and bringing home all the big trophies. But we can feel downright devastated if it seems like everyone else is a winner and we are always the last one selected in a pick-up ball game, can't we? I know, for you see, I still proudly root for the Chicago Cubs!

Our older-adult years are the perfect time to help others understand that we are always winners. This is the perfect time and place to announce to all that at our Baptism, the Lord placed a crown of life on our heads and announced, "I have made you a winner!" The trophy of Baptism will never tarnish, never fall off the wall, and never get stored in a cardboard box in the basement. We are winners because the Lord has chosen us, not because we have chosen Him. When we strike out in life or make an error or even fail to show up at the game, we are still pronounced winners by the Lord Himself. What a great message to give and share with all the other losers like us all around. Our sins say, "You lose." Christ's death and resurrection announce on the scoreboard of life, "You win!"

Philippians 3:14 states, "I press on toward the goal for the prize of the upward call of God in Christ Jesus." The great Good News is that we have already won the race because of what Christ has already done for us.

As older adults, we can be thankful for all our peers who are honored and recognized through their amazing accomplishments. This does not lessen our lives in any way. Celebrate with older people as they set home-run records, discover a cure for a dreaded disease, or invent something that will enable people to live healthier lives. As they go along in their calling, let us also go along in our calling to serve and care for people in the name of the healing Christ—and to enjoy life on the way, even if that means skydiving. Our accomplishments may not hit the front page, but our ministry to others will reach the hearts and lives of the people around us.

I remember a pastor friend who had become depressed because he felt he was not serving the Lord as best he could. Other churches were growing, and his was stumbling along, with very little growth in numbers. Another associate of ours listened intently to the pastor's laments and suggested that perhaps the Lord had not called this pastor to serve a large church and minister to thousands of people in his lifetime. Instead, perhaps the Lord was calling this pastor to be faithful to his flock, to his family, and to the people close around him. Good counsel! This does not mean that we should not expand our ministry fields or reach out to save the world, but it does mean that we are all called to be faithful in sharing our gifts and lives with others wherever we are. In this way, we allow the Spirit to work in and through us, and we are affirmed in our faith in the One who saves.

Have you made out your bucket list yet? If so, check it again. Do consider traveling all over the earth to see the wonders of the world, if you yearn for that type of experience. However, let me also suggest that you add to your list some very doable experiences as well, such as these:

- Smile at all the children you meet today.

- Never miss a chance to say "I love you" to those who mean the most to you.

- Say thanks to the basketball coach who is spending loads of time trying to teach your grandchild to shoot baskets.

- Take time to mentor and coach one of the greatest "wonders" of the world: children.

- Visit someone older than you, and sit and listen to all the wonder-filled stories he or she has to tell.

Go ahead and add to this list as you become famous in your own right, living and sharing and celebrating the gifts and the faith that the Lord has given you.

You are a winner. Continue to walk in your Baptism. You might even want to try skydiving, at least twice!

CHAPTER THIRTY-SEVEN

PARAPROSDOKIANS AND AGING

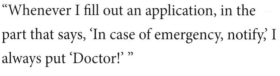

> "Whenever I fill out an application, in the
> part that says, 'In case of emergency, notify,' I
> always put 'Doctor!' "
>
> (Author unknown)

Have you ever heard of the word paraprosdokian? Me neither! It does, however, have a lot in common with the process of aging. Now, before you skip this section and move on, at least give me a chance to plead my case. Paraprosdokian is defined as a two-part figure of speech, a sentence or phrase in which the second part is contradictory, unexpected, or even shocking. This technique is typically used to make a joke. For example, "Where there's a will, I want to be in it!"

Here are a few more of my favorite paraprosdokians:

- If I agreed with you, we'd both be wrong.

- We never really grow up; we only learn how to act in public.

- The last thing I want to do is hurt you. But it's still on my list.

- Light travels faster than sound. This is why some people appear bright until you hear them speak.

- A clear conscience is the sign of a fuzzy memory.

- You do not need a parachute to skydive. You only need a parachute to skydive twice.

- You're never too old to learn something wrong.

- I didn't say it was your fault. I only said I was blaming you.

So what's the point, you ask? Simply this: The aging process has a lot in common with the concept of paraprosdokians. Growing older is perceived by many to be a negative experience. "Stay young"; "Go for the gusto"; "Always be young at heart"; "Oh, to be young again"—these are just a few phrases that strongly imply that growing older is something we should try to avoid. The focus of this book is, instead, "Guess what, folks? We aren't going to avoid it! Instead, by the grace of God, we embrace it, celebrate it, and live it boldly." No need even to try to avoid it; rather, we see and share it as a gift from God. We are empowered to live our lives not in the cultural perception of *old* but in the scriptural value of *bold*!

Just like our new word *paraprosdokian*, we need to read the whole sentence before we understand what is said. The aging process allows us to be able to read (that is, live) the entire message so that we receive the surprising and unexpected message at the end. In this sense, the message of aging is the creative, celebrative, and often humorous experiences that we can only fully understand as we grow older.

Life is full of surprising and unexpected experiences, just like paraprosdokians. One of the gifts of growing older is that we are better able to appreciate life to the full. So many things make better sense as we look back and see how the Lord has been working in and through us since our Baptism. The first part of our life, like the beginning of a sentence, can be misunderstood and unclear. The latter part of our life, just like our new word *paraprosdokian*, makes the whole experience more understandable and clear.

Rachel, one of our granddaughters, sent us this note recently: "God might not give you what you want when you want it, but He will give you what you need when you need it." Well said, indeed!

Another component of paraprosdokians is that they are often used to communicate humor. I like that concept as it applies to our aging process as well. Granted, you and I know all too well of the pains and pressures and problems we all face. We cannot and should not try to deny these "uh-ohs"; rather, we deal with them by remembering and reviewing the big "aha" of Easter. That is something to celebrate every day! Because we take our relationship with our Lord very seriously, we are able to take lightly both ourselves and the situations in which we find ourselves, in the name of the Lord.

Paul's words in 1 Thessalonians 5:16–18 come to mind here: "Rejoice always, pray without ceasing, give thanks in all circumstances; for this is the will of God in Christ Jesus for you." A couple things jump out of this text for me. First, the Lord is not saying give thanks *for* all things but rather *in* all things. We do not and cannot give thanks for all of the messes and muddles in which we find ourselves; nevertheless, we are able, by the power of the Holy Spirit, to give thanks in all situations. Second, when I hear that we are to "rejoice always," in my "uh-oh" times I might blurt out, "You have to be kidding!" Hearing the words "rejoice always" changes our whole attitude, our whole mindset toward life as a gift from the Lord. Such a change is an affirmation of the faith that is within us, faith that is ours because of what Christ has already done; it is not as a command that we "got to" do. When we compare our faith life as we age to understanding the end of a sentence, as we do with paraprosdokians, we begin to grasp the joy and celebration that is ours every day, especially in humorous ways.

One last observation: Some of the dictionaries I checked did not list the word *paraprosdokian*. My spell-checker did not acknowledge this word either. Aha! I smell a conspiracy! Perhaps this is indicative of the culture of the day and its unwillingness to accept the fact or to confirm the truth that the aging process is indeed a most positive force in our lives. As we age, we grow in faith and knowledge that the Lord is blessing us through our years from beginning to end. Yes, we can and will continue to celebrate God's gift of aging and see the humor in it as well, from start to finish.

Let us try just one more paraprosdokian: "I used to be indecisive. Now I'm not so sure!"

CHAPTER THIRTY-EIGHT

DOWNSIZING? NO, UPSIZING!

Humble yourselves before the Lord,
and He will lift you up.

(James 4:10 NIV)

A friend of mine claims that the worst invention ever made was the closet. If we had no closets, we would have no space to store all of the stuff that we accumulate over the years, and therefore we would have less stuff. Makes sense, doesn't it?

Your friends and mine continue to downsize as they age, trying to rid their homes of all the extra clutter. We might even try to sell a home and purchase a smaller one (if the banks allow). Stories and articles abound about how to simplify our lives by doing with less, especially because many people need to cut down on expenses and monthly bills. All this makes good sense, but to look at it another way, I strongly suggest that while we are downsizing, we also make every effort to upsize.

To upsize means to look up to affirm and acknowledge the strong presence of the Lord in our lives. To upsize means first to acknowledge that it is the Lord who provides all of our material possessions, even those we do not need, even those that have been hiding in our basement for ten years. To upsize means to joyfully share the gifts we receive with people who lack much in their bodily needs. As one pastor remarked, "Accept your fatness, and help skinny people get fat!" He obviously was not referring to physical traits but rather to the differences between the haves and the have-nots in our world.

The more we older adults look up to the Lord, the more it becomes clear to us that we are blessed by our possessions so we can be blessings to others. In fact, one way to rid our closets of stuff we do not use or need is to support local and worldwide ministries. These ministries help others not only to "get fat" but also to come to know the Lord Jesus Christ. Now, that really helps lift people up in the Lord!

Pope John XXIII wrote, "The older I grow the more clearly I perceive the dignity and the winning beauty of simplicity in thought, conduct and speech: a desire to simplify all that is complicated and to treat everything with the greatest naturalness and clarity" (*Journal of a Soul*, trans. Dorothy White [New York: Image Books, 1965], 278–79).

Romans 9:16–17 takes this slant on upsizing: "It depends not on human will or exertion, but on God, who has mercy. For the Scripture says to Pharaoh, 'For this very purpose I have raised you up, that I might show My power in you, and that My name might be proclaimed in all the earth.' " That same Lord has raised us up for that very purpose: to lift up the cross of Christ with our lives and possessions, right here and right now.

God in Christ is the one who enables us to look up. To upsize is first to acknowledge where our gifts come from and then to use these gifts to raise up others.

Continue to downsize and simplify your lifestyle. It is the healthy and correct thing to do. Skip the next special sale. No need to buy all those Christmas gifts for the grandchildren. Clean out your cupboards, and regularly take food and clothing to the food pantry in town. Contribute to ministry causes throughout the world. In order to enable others to upsize, we certainly can downsize; in the process, remind yourself and those around you that the Lord lifts us up as we are good stewards of His gifts to us. The apostle Paul has some great uplifting words for us in Colossians 2:6–7: "Therefore, as you received Christ Jesus the Lord, so walk in Him, rooted and built up in Him and established in the faith, just as you were taught, abounding in thanksgiving."

As we grow older, we have greater appreciation for all that the Lord has given to us throughout our previous years—probably more so than we could ever imagine. Those undeserved blessings we might have taken for granted in our earlier years, our experiences and faith allow us to be more grateful for as we age. We are able to make better choices, share more blessings, and focus more on what life in the Lord is all about. That is just another blessing of growing older: to be able to rid our minds and lives of the stuff that gets in the way of our faith and hope in the Lord.

I am ready to upsize my life in the Lord. How about you?

(I still think that the closet is the worst item ever created!)

CHAPTER THIRTY-NINE

WEE, WE, WHEE— ALL THE WAY HOME!

Older adults are caught in a world fixated on the worries, woes, and wars of life, both globally as well as in our own lives. Just last night, watching the evening news, I was struck by the irony of the news commentator saying, "Good Evening," and then proceeding to tell me why it wasn't.

Recent studies also point out that worship attendance is down; fewer and fewer confirmands are visible in their congregations six months after they publicly profess their faith in the Lord; denominational headquarters continue to reduce the number of staff positions; Lutheran schools are shrinking and closing. It's enough to make one feel insecure, impotent, unnecessary, and certainly worthless, to say the least.

Let's call this the "wee" factor of life. You and I can often feel that we are alone in our ministries as we try to make the world right. You and I can feel separated from one another as failures fall among previous failures. You and I can feel lonely and forgotten because of our sins and because of the way we mess things up in our family, our school, our congregation, and our personal lives. Yes, there is a lot of "wee-ness" going around these days: a sense that you and I are not important, not valuable, and not successful, and that we have very little to share. People of all ages have this dreaded "wee" sickness. It's called sin. After all, the needs are so great and other people have so much more going for them and so much more to share. I often feel like a zero, a nothing, a cipher. I am just another Zacchaeus—a "wee" little person.

But, there is hope for us "wee" people. Yes, indeed! The Lord brings us down from our lofty perches and brings us together as His "we" people. It's called the Church—the holy huddle, the grace place, the shalom zone, the friendly flock. In our Baptism, God takes the "wee-ness" of our lives and brings us through the font to mark us with His sign through water and the Word. To paraphrase John Donne, "No one is an island; we are all connected by the water of Baptism" (see John Donne, "Meditation XVII," *Devotions upon Emergent Occasions*, 1623). Thus, "wee" become "we"!

The Church confirms in us, through Christ, that life is not about "me" but rather about "we." When one of us suffers, we all suffer. When one of us rejoices, we all rejoice. "We" people live by grace that takes away our "wee-ness," even in the midst of our worries, woes, and wars. This grace binds us together for the warfare ahead of us. The "we" people of God move into the "wee-ness" of the world because we are one in Christ Jesus. To be alive is to be broken by sin and to know in faith that God in Christ graces us with His love and forgiveness.

"We" people have as their ministry motto, "Get over it, and get on with it!" "We" people know that it is not our "wee-ness" that we boast about; rather, it is by our "we-ness" that we live and serve other "wee" people around us. We become confident, bold, and courageous. We hear Paul saying to Timothy and to us, "God gave us a spirit not of fear but of power and love and self-control" (2 Timothy 1:7).

There is even more good news to share: Our response to God's love in Christ is a great big "whee!" We are now empowered to celebrate our faith; we become affirmed through others' gifts and support. We share our gifts with others and become strong people of faith, reaching out with a "whee" sense of celebrating life to the fullest, bringing health and hope to the "wee" people and the "we" people of the world.

Our motto becomes "whee-ness." We are the people of God. We can sing and shout, even when we do not feel like singing or shouting, because "The LORD has done great things for us; we are glad" (Psalm 126:3).

You see, our "we-ness" and our "whee-ness," in the midst of our "wee-ness," is not about us; it is about what God in Christ has already done for us. Even when we want to give up, run from life, and climb back up to our secure spot in a sycamore tree, we hear the gentle voice of a loving Father wooing us to come back down to earth again, back to the realities of life and death, jostles and joys, worries and woes, to the place where He has put us—and that place is right here and right now.

Christ's resurrection is the great "whee" of life. It takes our "wee-ness" and connects us to others to make a "we" Church, the Body of Christ, even when we know that the "Good evening" from the newscast is really not telling the whole story.

Matthew 28:8 clinches it for us "we" people when we hear again and again the Easter message: "They departed quickly from the tomb with fear and great joy"!

Yes, life is all about "we, wee, whee," all the way home.

(This chapter appeared as "Multiplying Ministries . . . Wee, We, Whee All the Way Home," by Rich Bimler. *Lutheran Education Journal*, December 10, 2010. http//lej .cuchicago.edu/columns/multiplying-ministries%E2% 80%A6wee-we-whee-all-the-way-home/ [accessed January 4, 2012]. Reprinted by permission.)

CHAPTER FORTY

ONCE MORE WITH ATTITUDE

"No matter how serious your life requires you to be, everyone needs a friend to get goofy with."
(Attributed to Andy Rooney)

If you are reading this together with someone, turn to each other and say, "My, you're aging gracefully!" Go ahead, no one is looking! (If you are reading this alone, you may want to say this silently to yourself, lest someone hears you talking to yourself!)

Now, didn't that feel good? And it is the truth. You and I are aging gracefully, even with our aches and pains and wrinkles and pill pouches. We are aging well because the Lord is in us and with us, constantly loving and forgiving us. We are aging well because our faith in Christ does not depend on how we look or on how we feel; rather, our faith depends on what God has done for us through Christ's death and resurrection. We are the people of God, now and forever. Because of this, we are aging gracefully.

Throughout these pages, I have tried to make the case that there is a big gap in attitudes toward aging. There is huge difference, in my mind at least, between the terms *old* and *growing older*. A fine point, you may argue, but I do not think so.

The word *old* connotes "end, final, finish," and, in itself, perhaps appropriately so. The term *growing older* is a more active phrase that shows movement, life, and activity. *Growing older* means that we are actively involved in life, moving forward, and on the way, in the process. *Old* in this culture too often means that we once were young, that we are have-beens or perhaps even "never were's."

In the Bible, the word *old* is used around 363 times, whereas the word *older* is used only around 17 times. If you are wondering how I came to those numbers, I must admit it was during a time of the night recently when I should have been sleeping or doing something worthwhile instead of counting words in the Bible. Just to pursue this numbers' game a bit further, I also must add that the words *grow* and *growing* appear around 61 times.

But I digress. Certainly the word *old* is used appropriately in many contexts. We love to sing "The Old Rugged Cross"; we gather with old friends; we recall the good old days. The list goes on and on. My argument is only that if the word *old* locks us into a mindset that says *old* is synonymous with "over and done for," we may fail to see the beauty and fullness of life in the Lord Jesus through all the years of our lives.

Another example: I was singing the hymn "Greet the

Rising Sun" a few months ago, and I came to the line, "As I teach the young And esteem the old" (*LSB* 871:2, © Stephen P. Starke). I like the tune and the text of this hymn. The only concern I have, in this one instance, is that this little phrase may give the impression that it is our role only to teach the young and only to esteem the old; in other words, it gives the perception that active and lively young people are to be taught, whereas old folks are simply to be esteemed. In defense of these words, it is accurate that the Scriptures describe older adults as wise and deserving respect. Listen to Job 12:12: "Wisdom is with the aged, and understanding in length of days." I understand that and I accept it, but not at the expense of locking our minds and attitudes into a negative, pathological view of older people, because we happen to be growing older gracefully in the Lord.

Many years ago, in my book *Angels Can Fly Because They Take Themselves Lightly* (Concordia Publishing House, 1992), I quoted Rabbi Cohen as he shared his thoughts on life. I felt it was appropriate as he suggested, in jest, a new approach to living. Here it is:

"Life is tough. It takes up a lot of your time, all your weekends, and what do you get in the end? . . . I think that the life cycle is all backwards. You should die first, get it out of the way. Then you live twenty years in an old-age home. You get kicked out when you're too young. You get a gold watch. You go to work. You work forty years until you're young enough to enjoy your retirement. You go to college. You party until you are ready for high school. You go to grade school. You become a little kid. You play. You have no responsibilities. You become a little baby. You go back into the womb. And you finish up as a gleam in somebody's eye!" (Rabbi Cohen, as quoted in *Angels Can Fly Because They Take Themselves Lightly*, p. 122).

My, have my thoughts changed since then. Call it growing older, but the above paragraph does not view growing older in a positive way at all. Clever and cute, right. Does it have a point? Perhaps. However, to see life and death as something "to get it out of the way," to deny living life to the full, is an attitude that needs changing and changing quickly.

To be fair to the above quote and the rationale for using it, it did make the point that the more pagan a society gets, the more boring its people become. It emphasized that the light of Christ is needed to lighten up the world and that people of God in Christ are people filled with a bold mischievousness of the Gospel. I still certainly buy that!

Enjoy the joy-filled journey of growing older. Please join me in being sensitive to how we perceive, how we label, and how we live out our lives as God's people, at whatever age we happen to be. Sing and celebrate birthdays of eight-year-olds, eighteen-year-olds, and certainly eighty-year-olds. Affirm and confirm your faith in how you live and how you portray others. Help others realize that a life in Christ at any age is not a problem-free zone. Help people around you grasp that the process of overcoming adversity and dealing with pains, problems, and panic often becomes the most rewarding and blessed experience you will ever have.

May the Lord continue to bless us as we grow older gracefully in the Lord!

CHAPTER FORTY-ONE

AN AGING LITANY

"When we live from God's breath we recognize with joy that the same breath that keeps us alive is also the source of life for our brothers and sisters"

(Henri Nouwen, *With Open Hands*, second revised edition [Notre Dame, IN: Ave Maria Press, 1972, 2006], p. 55)

Aging allows us to reflect on all of the hundreds of people who have touched our lives through the past waning years. Aging allows us to remember parents, grandparents, teachers, pastors, neighbors, classmates, colleagues at work, and even friends we've met in the grocery stores of life. Right now is a great time to stop and say thanks to the Lord for placing these people into our lives.

One of the miracles of these people who intersect our lives is that each one of them brought at the right time something we needed—a smile, a laugh, a caution, a ride, a friend, a nudge, a no or a yes, a word of counsel, a hug, a phone call, a silence, a sigh, even an "aha."

Reflect for a moment and name some of those people who touched you in your early years. How about in your young adult years? How about right now? Now turn it around and think of people who, if they were doing this same exercise, would mention your name. Go ahead, do not be shy or humble about it; be proud that you have touched someone with the hand and heart of the Lord.

What will today bring to you and to others? Who will reach out to touch you in a special way this day? Watch for them, and acknowledge them. As you watch for people responding to your needs, look around to see others who need your touch and, through it, God's touch as well. I call these "God sightings." God sightings are how we see the Lord living in and through us each day as we reach out to others and others reach out to us. This outreach happens because the Lord has already reached out His hands on the cross and has touched us through His death and resurrection.

Share the following litany from Herb Brokering, a saint who has touched so many lives with God's grace and love throughout the world. Thank you, Herb. When I think of you, I give God thanks, in the name of Jesus!

When my wings were wounded
You gave me a steady wind to help them fly;
When my voice lost its song
You gave me a new tune to sing;

When my spirit fell
You said my name in a special way;

When a cloud covered my sun
You showed me a star in the dark;

When tears blinded my seeing
You wiped them with a soft smile;
When I lost my way home
You went with me to find it; When it was too
quiet and slow
You helped me pull out all the stops;
When I didn't know what to do next
You served a casserole with candles;

When I couldn't find my garden
You sent flowers to my altar;
When my heart was empty
You filled it with a fugue;

When my life was thirsty for something spe-
cial
You poured me a tiny cup of wine;
When I gave You something funny
You took it as a prize;

When I was overjoyed with a dream
You wanted to see it too;
When I lost my place in believing
You repeated familiar words I knew;

When the waves were too high and deep
You stayed beside me;
When my feet could not take another step
You surprised me with a new way to go;

When I was bored
You asked about another part of my story;
When I didn't want to be there
You ushered me in;

When I felt too old or little
You held up a child for me to cheer on;
When I was tired of giving
You asked me to receive;

When I think of You
I give thanks.

(Dr. Herb Brokering, used by permission)

CHAPTER FORTY-TWO

PAINS, PERCEPTIONS, AND PROMISE

"Do not cast me off in the time of old age;
forsake me not when my strength is spent."

(Psalm 71:9)

One of the most challenging things about growing older is dealing with the pains and agonies of our bodies slowing down, closing down, and deteriorating. We all have had these shaky and humbling experiences, either from our own bodies or because of the pains of loved ones around us. Psalm 71:9 is a plea and a prayer than many of us have echoed: Lord, do not leave me. I need You now more than ever.

Often, the pain continues. The medicine increases. The mobility lessens. The hope grows dimmer. The caregivers give. The care receivers receive. Is this what growing older is really all about?

To this question, we need to give an honest answer, and the answer is yes. Yes, our bodies will fail. Our hopes will dampen. Our daily needs will increase and we will become more dependent on others. The pain will often increase too.

The perception is, at least to many, that hope is gone,

that another life may soon be over, that as we hear at funerals, "ashes to ashes, dust to dust," that the end is coming.

Our pain and our perception of pain have much to do with our outlook and attitude toward life. If we consider pain as something to be removed, something that is abnormal, something we must conquer, then we are in a losing battle. If growing older means we must do everything possible to deny pain now or the advent of pain later, we will not win this battle either. If growing older equals pain and more pain, why in the world am I looking forward to growing older? I want out—now!

A recent study fits in nicely here. Researchers went about exploring older adult's stereotypes of aging based upon their personal experiences as well as the experiences of others. They tested whether or not one's perception of aging influenced falls, hospitalizations, or the need for assistance with everyday activities. The findings showed that 38 percent of those studied held a negative perception of their own aging, and three years later, a negative perception of their own health was strongly associated with difficulties in basic and independent activities of daily living. Other factors associated with negative perception of aging were low income, living alone, chronic medical conditions, and depression. According to this study, then, how we perceive our own health and aging directly affects our daily living situations and behaviors. (The Journals of Gerontology, Series B; Psychological Sciences, 66B(6), 675–685, November 2011.)

The writer of Psalm 90 might have been having one of those days also. He appeals to God for sympathy: "All our days pass away under Your wrath; we bring our years to an end like a sigh" (v. 9).

No way, my aging body shouts. No moaning and sighing for me. I choose to finish my life with a big hooray and even a bigger "aha." That still is in the plan, of course, as the Lord constantly brings His promise of life to us.

Our lives seem so short according to God's sense of time. Why do we need to spend these fleeting days suffering and moaning? Verse 12 records a plea, a request from the writer that believers still echo: "Teach us to number our days that we may get a heart of wisdom." Now we're talking the talk as we walk the walk of the promise of our Lord!

I hear in Psalm 90 many of the thoughts and words I have spent thinking and praying about life, suffering, and death. The psalmist catches me, and perhaps you, reiterating my own worries and struggles. Like the psalmist, we shout out, or perhaps just whisper, "You have set our iniquities before You, our secret sins in the light of Your presence" (v. 8). Let's face it. When we feel pain and aches and our abilities slow down, we do not have much left in us to deal with this failing situation. As one devotion reads, "I plead with God to cover my debts with forgiveness, afraid that the words of absolution are for everyone except me or that their grace expires with time. These prayers rise not like incense, but reek of insecurity and doubt" (Meta Herrick Carlson, St. John's Lutheran Church, Minneapolis, Minnesota).

The pains are there, and they will continue. Our perception of life is that we deserve something better than what we are experiencing. God's promise trumps both the pain and the perceptions. I can see the Lord bringing His comfort and hope to us through Word and Sacrament and through those special people who surround us: family, friends, doctors, nurses, pastors, and caregivers, among others.

Life is short, says the Lord. Why do you choose to spend it suffering for things I have already forgiven and things Christ has already done for you? See the cross and the empty tomb? It is there in front of you. And it will always be there, in Jesus' name!

CHAPTER FORTY-THREE

DYING WELL

> "I had been taught all my life how to die, but
> no one had ever taught me how to grow old."
>
> (Billy Graham, *Nearing Home: Life, Faith, and Finishing Well* [Nashville, TN: Thomas Nelson, Inc., 2011], p. 93)

Life in the Lord is all about living well, aging well, and dying well. That is life in the Lord! The Scriptures pound out the message that Jesus went around proclaiming, teaching, and healing. Someone once said that one-third of all of Jesus' ministry was about making people well. Another expert chimed in and suggested instead that three-thirds of Jesus' ministry was about bringing wellness to people, through His life, suffering, death, and resurrection. I like that concept!

Have you noticed lately that our society still has difficulty using the word *death* in conversations? Our culture is good at denying that people age gracefully as well as that people die. Instead, people "pass on" or just "pass," or they are "not with us any longer," or they are "in a better place." Years ago, I was speaking at a conference, and someone asked where Hazel was. Without thinking much about it, I simply said, "Oh, she's gone," meaning that she was out of town visiting some friends. Immediately, the person responded in shock, "Oh, I didn't hear. I'm so sorry. When did she pass?" Later on, we had a chuckle about it, which is probably the best way to deal with it. Perhaps I need to be more careful with my terms! (And by the way, Hazel is back.)

Recently, I read this wry remark: "Death is the nation's number one killer." It is certainly hard to argue with that statement. However, the problem is that many people in our society still do not behave as if they understand that death is inevitable. Death is a constant for all of us.

If we are unable or unwilling to learn to die well, it will be hard for us to learn how to live well and to age well. Our congregations need to be seen as places where a culture of resurrection is taught and proclaimed from the cradle to the grave. How many funerals have your grandchildren attended? How many visitations have they experienced? My hunch is that many young people have not been exposed to places where dying well is taught and experienced.

Dying is not a pleasant topic for most people. Remember my friend who likes to say, "My goal in life is to live forever. And so far, so good!"? Our society seems to imply that if we do not talk about death or plan for death, it will simply not happen. But, it will certainly happen, and we can't prevent it!

I've heard it said that if you're not busy living, then

you're busy dying. I disagree. I strongly believe that one who is not busy living is not busy dying either! Living well, aging well, and dying well are all parts of a trinity that cannot be separated.

In the excellent book *The Art of Dying*, the author, Rob Moll, helps the reader capture the deeply Christian practice of dying well. He claims that modern medicine has drastically changed the way we die:

> One study found that most elderly people are diagnosed as having a disease three years before it will eventually end their lives. On top of that a Rand study found that "Americans will usually spend two or more of their final years disabled enough to need someone else to help with routine activities of daily living because of chronic illness." (Joanne Lynn and David M. Adamson, "Living Well at the End of Life: Adapting Health Care to Serious Chronic Illness in Old Age," a RAND Corporation White Paper, 2003; as quoted by Rob Moll, *The Art of Dying* [Downers Grove, IL: InterVarsity Press, 2010], p. 27)

This reality has major implications for the need for more family caregivers, not to mention the ministries that are so needed to care and comfort those who are disabled. I can better understand now a comment that Billy Graham had made in his book *Nearing Home*, where he quotes a friend as saying, "People either seem to get better or get bitter as they grow older" (*Nearing Home*, p. 88). What a challenge we have to be available, to be there, to bring health and hope to people, and to move them from their bitterness to their betterness, all in the name of the healing Christ!

Another concept of the process of dying comes from a doctor in Chicago. He says that he hopes to die slowly so that he can spend time with family and friends and be able to confess and share his faith in the Lord. The key challenge for each of us is how we live well, age well, and die well, while affirming and celebrating the love and forgiveness we have in Jesus Christ. Exciting times ahead!

Through faith, "We know that for those who love God all things work together for good" (Romans 8:28). Through the living, aging, and dying process, we find strength in Christ, not only to endure trouble, problems, and hardships, but also to overcome them. When trouble comes, we do not despair, blame ourselves for our lack of faith, or blame God. Rather, we find our strength in the Word and Sacraments and acknowledge that as sinful people we are subject to the inevitable storms of life that face us all. Yet through all the turmoil of time and testing, Jesus claims us for His own, forever and forever and forever. That is a very long time!

The following story has been attributed to Dr. Billy Graham, which he shared with a group of people who were honoring him for his worldwide ministries throughout his life. He said he was reminded of Albert Einstein who was once travelling from Princeton on a train. The conductor came by to punch the tickets of the passengers. When he came to Einstein, Einstein reached into his pocket but could not find his ticket. "That's okay, Dr. Einstein," the conductor said, "I know who you are. I'm sure you have a ticket. Don't worry about it."

The conductor continued down the aisle punching tickets. As he was moving to the next car, he turned around and saw Dr. Einstein on his hands and knees looking under the seat for his ticket. The conductor rushed back and pleaded, "Dr. Einstein, don't worry, I know who you are. You don't need a ticket." Einstein looked at him and said, "Young man, I, too, know who I am. What I don't know is where I am going!"

Dr. Graham closed his remarks by strongly sharing his faith with these words: "I want you to remember this: You and I not only know who we are, we also know where we are going!"

Life without the Lord is like an unsharpened pencil: it has no point. We live well, we age well, and we die well, because the Lord has brought us His wellness through the death and resurrection of Jesus Christ! We are well, whether we look like it, feel like it, or act like it. We are well in the Lord!

Pastor Herb Brokering clinches it for us as we celebrate aging as the only way to live:

> Lord, send me a surprise.
> One that catches me off guard
> and makes me wonder.
> Like Easter.
>
> Send me a resurrection
> when everything looks dead
> and buried.
> Send me light
> when the night seems too long.
> Send me spring
> when the cold and frozen season
> seems endless.
> Send me a new idea
> when my mind is empty.
> Send me a thing to do
> when I am just waiting around.
> Send me a new friend
> when I am alone.
> Send me peace
> when I'm afraid.
> Send me a future

when it looks hopeless.
Send me Your resurrection
when I die, Jesus.

(Used by permission)

CHAPTER FORTY-FOUR

GOT CHANGE?

"Change and decay in all around I see; O
Thou who changest not, abide with me."

("Abide with Me," *LSB* 878:4)

For years, I have known that one thing is constant in life: change. This is especially so for older adults, who are flooded and challenged with the advice and counsel to change. I believe in this encouragement and philosophy. Of course, older adults need to change in the ways we do and think and see things.

Remember that saying, "If you change the way you look at things, the things you look at change"? Well spoken. Good advice. But now, what do we do with it?

Looking at today's society, you can get the impression that if we do not change our thinking or our behaviors, then we are out of touch or living only in the past. I refute those charges, strongly, loudly and clearly! As a matter of fact, one of the major roles of older adults in society is to remind the next generations that roots and traditions are essential for growth and healthy living, today and in the future. Trees and plants grow because of their root systems.

Pull out the roots, and living things perish. The task of keeping younger people's roots intact is a major responsibility for older adults.

On the other hand, another concern about change is that it can appear as though we no longer live in God's world because of all of the negative changes that are occurring in our life. It is as if God has abandoned His world and that, like Elvis, He "has left the building." Not so, say we older people, not so! Genesis is still accurate when it proclaims that "In the beginning, God created the heavens and the earth. . . . And behold, it was very good" (Genesis 1:1, 31). Sin came into the world, of course, but the sin of mankind, which includes your sins and mine, by the way, has been crushed by the power of God at work in the world through His Son, Jesus Christ. Sin is still very evident and prevalent in our world and in us, but the victory is won! Remember, we live on this side of the resurrection. John 3:16 reminds us that "God so loved the world." He gave His only Son to die and rise for everyone—not just for the Church, but for the whole world.

The quote on the previous page, from the brilliant hymn "Abide with Me," might be one small example of how even the Church can sometimes give the perception that all change is negative. I agree to a point with the hymnwriter that "change and decay in all around I see," but by placing the words *change* and *decay* together, it might seem that change equals decay, which is probably not what the hymn-writer intended to imply. If you and I see that change in fact does equal decay, then we are all in deep trouble.

Of course, you and I love change, right? I have never regretted the invention of indoor plumbing! Praise God for the invention of air conditioning! I thank the Lord for that little device, the cell phone, on which I can mysteriously hear my grandkids speaking to me. Let us also not forget that thanks to the Wright brother's ingenuity we no longer have to wait for the next stagecoach to get to Nebraska. We don't even have to get off the couch to change the channel on our new flatscreen TV.

So what do we do with the concept of change? We had best get used to it, because change is constant, whether we like it or not. As older adults, we are in a position to help ourselves as well as others deal with change in the midst of the Christ-life that never changes. Here are some coping mechanisms to consider:

1. Remember that Christ is the changeless one. It almost sounds trite in some ways, but it is true in all ways. He is the beginning and the end, the Alpha and the Omega, the first and the last. This is just not holy hype, it is holy hope! Take a look again at our hymn stanza: "O Thou who changest not, abide with me" (*LSB* 878:4).

2. Be ready to accept the inevitability of change. That is not to say that we will experience or even need to accept all changes. It does mean that instead of only being against something, perhaps we can more effectively be for something.

For example, I struggle with how some people dress for worship on Sunday morning. I also realize that we are judged not by what we wear but by the faith that the Lord is growing within us. How do I deal with this? Not always well, thank you. I do, however, wear a sport coat and tie to worship, in the midst of the tank tops and cut-offs. I do tell people, gently, that I am surprised that many people in today's culture only dress up for funerals and sometimes for weddings. To me, how we dress shows respect to those we are with, and we give people value and a sense of worth in so doing. I do not plan to win this battle, but at least I will go down with my tie on.

More serious is an attitude I sense about the need for worship in today's society. I am troubled at the lack of worship attendance among God's people. How do I accept this change? By praying, by trying to understand the culture, and by being respectful to the feelings of others, but I also deal with it by sharing my feelings and concerns about the situation.

3. Respect the past and learn from it. This is not our grandparents' world, and for many reasons, I am glad. I do miss driving an Oldsmobile, but I will get over it. The older I become, the more important traditions are becoming—for example, Christmas dinner with the whole family. I am learning that the whole Bimler family will have fewer and fewer opportunities to do things together because of schedules and ages and travel and new relationships. Instead of feeling badly about not being able to have all fifteen of us around the table at holidays, I am changing my expectations, and I try to thank the Lord for all of the past family experiences we have had together. Do I like this reality? No, but I am trying to learn and adjust to it. We can have all fifteen together on another day. And at least we have fewer dishes to wash and fewer rooms to clean during the holidays!

4. Be willing to adapt. We need to recalculate our expectations to deal with change, as our GPS narrator says to us as we are driving in traffic. Older adults need to be more open to changes along the roads of life. Sometimes we fail to turn when we should, so we recalculate. Sometimes we are not

listening closely enough to people around us, and we need to recalculate. Sometimes we think our agenda and directions are the best for everyone, but we need to recalculate. To be open to change by recalculating our expectations and our desired outcomes is a very healthy and necessary way to live in today's world. Perhaps GPS really means "God's Promise Sends"!

5. Believe in God's promise and the future. Jeremiah 29:11 is such a powerful verse: "For I know the plans I have for you, declares the LORD, plans for welfare and not for evil, to give you a future and a hope." The future is not in our hands, and hooray for that! The future might look bleary and somber and fearful. The future may not look pretty at all. Nevertheless, God's promise is sure. God's promise is with us. God is with us, and we shout out, "Immanuel!"

Change can certainly be disabling, depressing, and even disastrous. However, it is only so if or when we forget about God's promise that He will never leave us or forsake us. "My hope is built on nothing less," as we often so boldly sing (*LSB* 575:1). The Lord is our hope, and He is here, and that is the fact of our faith in Christ Jesus!

As you and I deal with change, let us first rejoice in the presence of the Lord in us. After that, as a wise sage once said, "It's all small stuff!" As we center on Christ's relationship in us, we can also adjust to life's challenges and changes by getting enough physical exercise (walk, walk, and walk some more!), keeping our minds active, eating appropriately, reducing environments that cause us stress (staying out of Chicago traffic is one I am working on!), and being with other people, especially the friendly ones!

Got change? You bet. Can we deal with it? Of course. In a world where even carpenters are resurrected, anything is possible.

On days when I am stressed, when I need to lower my expectations about myself and others, when I am struggling through some of the "uh-ohs" of life, I try to remember Matthew's account of that first Easter, especially Matthew 28:8: "So [the women] departed quickly from the tomb with fear and great joy." Are we afraid? Yes. Are we filled with joy? Yes, because of Christ's forgiveness for all the messes we make in life.

How stunning! How powerful! How just like us! How life-changing!

CHAPTER FORTY-FIVE

A CALL TO CHANGE
THE WAY WE AGE

We have a lot of work to do, we aging ones! It will take our eager energies and our conscious commitments to bring about an attitude of change within our Church and society in the years ahead. However, if we do not do it, who will?

Of course, the good news in this process is that it is the Lord who works wonders and wows in our lives as we celebrate God's gift of aging.

In the book *Let There Be Laughter*, which my son and I wrote years ago, we quoted the sainted Henri Nouwen in his wonderful book *Creative Ministry*:

> When we are born, we become free to breathe on our own but lose the safety of our mother's body; when we go to school, we are free to join a greater society but lose a particular place in our family; when we marry, we find a new partner but lose the special tie we had with our parents; when we find work, we win our independence by making our own money

but lose the stimulation of teachers and fellow students; when we receive children, we discover a new world but lose much of our freedom to move; when we are promoted, we become more important in the eyes of others but lose the chance to take many risks; when we retire, we finally have the chance to do what we wanted but lose the support of being wanted.

(Henri Nouwen, *Creative Ministry* [New York: Image Books, 1971, 2003], p. 97)

This is our challenge in the years ahead. Our lives cannot be the "same old, same old" style of living. We cannot pine for the good old days and, by so doing, forget to notice that these, right now, are the good new days. We cannot bemoan all of what is going wrong in this world and then forget about doing what is right for this world. We can wallow in a perception that we somehow became the victims on our way to making a living and then lose the God-given opportunities to make a difference in life, right now, today. We cannot misquote Scripture by saying, "Here I am! Send . . . her." Rather, confidently and in faith, we proclaim loudly the words of Isaiah 6:8: "Here I am! Send me," even when we do not feel like it or act like it or look like it.

The years ahead for all of us will not be easy, but they will be blessed. As our population ages, as we all age together, more and more pressure will be upon you and me to live out our lives as gifts and blessings rather than as grouches and burdens. This will only begin as each of us thanks the Lord for His presence and for His promise to be with us to the end.

The years ahead will see gigantic growth in numbers of older adults. Remember, folks, it's clear that the Lord really does love us older people because He is making so many more of us. Right now there are over 110 million baby boomers and their parents, with over 2 trillion dollars in spending power. That is a lot of people and a lot of power! We will have more years to live, more gifts to give, and more people to forgive around us. Marketers will soon stop ignoring the over-sixty-five demographic and will finally understand that there still is power in numbers, even though we, as those numbers, are old. Churches will soon better understand that older adults are the centerpiece and the future of congregational life rather than the historical remnants of years gone by. I see a time when more and more congregations will have adult day care centers, classrooms for older people to tutor younger people of the community, staff persons specifically called to minister to and with older adults, and so many new and exciting ministry opportunities in which the old and the young can participate together, both locally and globally.

Here are a number of ways that we older people can come together in a "Call to Action" to change the way we age while at the same time changing the way people look at aging. These are shared not as a to-do list and something you "gotta" do, but rather as a "ta-da" list of possibilities from the resurrected Lord that we "get to" do:

1. Celebrate each day of your life as a gift from God. This is difficult to do, especially as we deal with our increasing pains, problems, and perplexities. Remind yourself each day that "We are the Lord's!" That is for sure!

2. Give your life away each day to someone else. We do this by looking for the lost, the least, the last, and the lonely around us. We also give our lives away by giving family and friends some of the things we have treasured over the years. Wrap up some of your favorite wall hangings, Christmas tree ornaments, and old dishes. Better to give your treasures away now than to have them sold at a garage sale after we die. The gift is in the giving!

3. Be vocal in your congregation and community about helping others see that aging is the only way to live. Help train and equip those younger than you to grasp better this attitude of aging that is so sorely needed.

4. Instead of waiting for people to come and find you when you feel lonely and alone, take the initiative

and go out and find others who also need friends and relationships in order to celebrate life together. When you see someone without a smile, give him one of yours!

5. Do something creative each day—something that might surprise even you. Start a journal, read a new book, learn a new skill, ride a bike, call someone just to say hello, make cookies for a neighbor, or go hang out at the local coffee shop and just watch people.

6. Be an advocate for older adults among your family, your congregation, and your community. No need to speak for all older adults, but at least speak for one of them: yourself. When you see and hear about older adults being left out and forgotten, become the divine irritant as you firmly and forgivingly point out that older adults are blessings rather than burdens.

7. Serve as a reality check for older people and their families. Point out how useless anti-aging cream really is. Speak positively for your peers when you hear others laughing at older people rather than laughing with them. Give your pastor some hints on how better to refer to older adults in sermon illustrations and in Bible classes through positive

stories and experiences. How we perceive older adults is so crucial to how we treat and refer to them.

8. Laugh at yourself! Start by looking in the mirror, with no clothes on. That should keep us chuckling for most of the day! What is precisely funny about each of us is that we take ourselves too seriously. Laughter is actually praising God because it allows human beings to be human and allows God to be God!

9. In order to help us laugh more at ourselves and with one another, be creative in how you look at life. Seek out little jokes, stories, and comic strips that speak directly to you. Tell these anecdotes to some people and wait for them to get it. If they do not understand what you are talking about, either pick new stories or find some happier friends. Here is just one example of how older adults can find fun in life: Look for signs and even bumper stickers that make you laugh. Here is a top ten list of bumper stickers for older adults that my son Bob developed:

The Top Ten Bumper Stickers for Older Adults

10. Wave if you love my driving!

9. My other car is a walker.

8. Caution: grandparent on board.

7. I may be slow, but I am ahead of you.

6. Honk all you want. I can't hear you anyway.

5. How's my driving? Call 1-800-WHO CARES?

4. Have you hugged your grandkids today?

3. What did Jesus say to the Chicago Cubs? "Don't do anything until I come back!"

2. Honor Roll student, class of 1951.

1. Follow me: I'm on my way to Bingo!

10. Look around you constantly to see how you can encourage more positive and realistic views of aging. Be proactive in changing your congregation's and society's perceptions of aging, starting with yourself.

11. Consider how you personally can rebrand aging in what you do and say. Do all you can to break down the stereotypes that some people have of being old. Be "old as in bold!" as you lightheartedly nudge people to reconsider how they look, speak, and act around older people. One of the best ways of doing

this is not to deny aging yourself. Shout out (figuratively speaking!) to people that you are proud to be older each day. Tell people your real age, whether they ask you or not. When someone says to you, "You look good for your age," simply acknowledge it and firmly tell this person that this is exactly how you are supposed to look at your age. Enjoy catching people stereotyping older people and then challenge yourself to enable them to see aging differently, in themselves and in others.

12. Search the Scriptures. Read the Psalms over and over and over. They truly speak the truth about the blessings and challenges of aging, and they point to the Lord, who is with us through all ages. Notice how many of the men and women in the Scriptures are older adults. What a reassurance that the Lord indeed works in and through people of all ages and is with us throughout our lives until He calls us home. Marvel again at how the Lord brings generations together in order for His will to be done and for His kingdom to come, right here, right now, in this place.

We have been called to action in our Baptism. We are called to action every day as the Lord provides us with another day to live life in Him to the full.

Remember again these words: "If you change the way you look at things, the thing you look at changes!"

Look out aging world! Look out, changing world! Here we come, in the name of the Lord!

Aging is the only way to live life in the Lord!

CHAPTER FORTY-SIX

A POSTSCRIPT
(OR, "GEE, I WISH I HAD INCLUDED THESE THOUGHTS SOONER!")

"Aging is the only way to live." What a great statement of joy and hope in living. The one thing all of us are doing together every day is aging. So, what do we do about it?

As we conclude this journey, here are a few final thoughts to share. Truth be told, I just do not remember if I shared these ideas in the previous pages or not!

We can either complain about all of the worries, woes, and wrinkles around us, or we can accept these realities and move on with our aging lives. I choose the latter option.

Life is given to us as a gift, and the gift of aging is something to celebrate each day. All too often, our society still sees aging as a burden. I prefer to see aging as a blessing! We can arise each morning groaning, "Oh, Lord, it's morning," or we can bounce out of bed (figuratively, anyway!), and exclaim, "Thanks, Lord, it's morning!" Yes, aging is the only way to live.

We older adults have so much to share and contribute to society as we live out our daily lives. No need to go around with an attitude of "Been there, done that." Instead, we can see our gifts and experiences and wisdom as opportunities to celebrate each day as a gift, as we seek ways to enjoy life by sharing an "attitude of gratitude" with those around us. For example, what one thing are you thankful for today? Name it, and then share it with others. It is the only way to live.

We older adults also need to laugh at ourselves more often. I do not know about you, but I often take myself too seriously. "Lighten up!" is a great mission statement for people our age. This brings to mind the story of a family who was very concerned about their eighty-year-old father who starting dating a seventeen-year-old high school student. One son was very upset; another one was too angry even to discuss it with his father. However, the daughter encouraged her brothers to think more positively about the situation. "Look at it this way," she suggested. "They're both seniors!" Yes, aging and laughing is the only way to live.

If you woke up this morning, it must mean that you still have a purpose in life to fulfill. Remember that old story about the guy who would get up each morning, check the obituary column to see if his name was listed, and if not, he would go back to bed? Probably not a good way to live life! I remember interviewing a one-hundred-year-old woman in Denver a few years ago. I asked her, "Lena, what is your secret of living to be one hundred years old?" After a long silence, Lena looked around, thought for a while, scratched her nose, and then with a smile, she said, "Well, I get up every morning!" Now that is what I call living! Oh, to celebrate life as Lena did!

Check out the signs around you today that affirm that aging is the only way to live. Look for the gifts of life and celebration in those you rub shoulders with today. Feel good about sharing the gifts you have as a senior adult with someone younger than you, or even someone older than you. Go out of your way to be that smiling senior to someone you meet. No need to bemoan the fact that you and I are older today than we were yesterday. Instead, celebrate this day as another day of life to give away. There is nothing wrong with remembering the "good old days," as long as we also remember that today is the start of a "good new day."

Embrace aging! It is a gift! Develop an attitude that affirms that we are not "getting old" but rather that we are "aging." It makes all the difference in how we approach each and every day in the Lord.

In a lighthearted yet serious way, we can profess and proclaim to one another:

"Get over it!" We are aging. Hooray!

"Get on with it!" Live life for all it is worth, starting today.

We can do this not because we "got to" but because we "get to," in the name of Jesus, our Lord and Savior!

May we pray each day, "Create in me a clean heart, O God, and renew a right spirit within me. Cast me not away from Your presence, and take not Your Holy Spirit from me. Restore to me the joy of Your salvation, and uphold me with a willing spirit" (Psalm 51:10–13).

And remember, "Until further notice, celebrate everything!" because aging is the only way to live!